Beautiful Black Women Don't Need Stupid
Black Men: They Need Beautiful
Black Love

By
Cornell Martin

ISBN: 978-1-4669-4816-7 (sc)
ISBN: 978-1-4669-4818-1 (hc)
ISBN: 978-1-4669-4817-4 (e)

Library of Congress Control Number: 2012913063

Trafford rev. 07/28/2012

www.trafford.com

North America & international
toll-free: 1 888 232 4444 (USA & Canada)
phone: 250 383 6864 ♦ fax: 812 355 4082

Contents

Beautiful Black Woman, my flower, my sky
My power is nothing without you
By my side
My spirit, my soul, my feelings
Inside
Should never be the cause
Of the tears that you cry
Hurt you—never
Sorry, if I ever did
Three words but eight letters
"I Love You"
That's what this is
Stupid—I once was
Black Love—I now chase
I'm not afraid of transparent liquid
Running down my face
I cry for you, would *die* for you
Your hand inside of my hand
Is similar to the sands
Of the earth traversed by man
Our love grains will never separate, never scatter
In my world, believe me
You're the *only* thing that matters

Cornell Martin
Ode of Black Love

Dedication

For Every Black Woman who is or has ever been fed up
with the stupid shit that so many Black Men do.
Each of you has a piece of my heart.
Cherish it like I cherish you.
This book is for *you*.
I *love* you!

Acknowledgements

God: None of this would be possible without you. Thanks for manipulating the events that caused my earthly father's seed to take root in my mother's womb. Thanks for all of the pain you have allowed me to experience on this material plane. If I could, I would *not* change a *thing*. You made me who I am, and I could *never* love another without loving you first!

My Publisher: For giving me the opportunity to creatively express myself by way of autonomous self-expression. You are doing a great service to humanity, and I will continue doing business with you one way or another for as long as God wills. We have not even scratched the surface of the kind of success that I envision. In time, you will see that my loyalty to you is unparalleled.

Shandreka and Eddison: For believing in me and supporting me throughout the years. Your love is obviously contagious, because love is all I feel when I either think of you or am in your presence. All I see is Beautiful Black Love when I look at you two love birds! Whenever I meet Mrs. Right, I want our love to be as potent as yours.

All of my nieces and nephews: I pray that you all find true love when you grow up. Sometimes the pathway to love is rocky, and sometimes it is smooth. If the former is more intense than the latter, then avoid that kind of love, because you do not need it. But if the latter is more intense than the former, then that is the kind of love I deem beautiful. *Always* seek beautiful love, and your lives will be joyously fulfilling.

Wendy Raquel Robinson: For being so damn down for your man! I respect you more than words can explain. He is so *blessed* to have you! Know that I will *always* consider you a goddess of the utmost quality. Your love for him inspires me.

Kerry Washington: From Standard Deviant's *¿Habla Espanol? Learning Spanish: The Basics* until now, you have never ceased to amaze me. Your innate thirst for Beautiful Black Love has been of great interest to both my soul and me. I wish that I could tickle your heart with a flower of love. No hay nada en este mundo que Usted no merece. Espero que lo encuentra el amor verdadero. Truly, you are worthy of nothing less!

Vivica A. Fox: Most men misunderstand you, which is, for the most part, the primary reason why the true love you seek currently eludes you. Like so many dudes have told me that they "respect my gangsta," I respect your *goddess*. If ever our paths cross, I believe we will both experience emotional fireworks. Keep searching for that love, girl! And when you find it, *hold on to it.*

Elise Neal: For being so damn *strong*. Heartbreak could *never* crush you! You are too real for most men. I know that you crave Beautiful Black Love, because I see it in your eyes, oozing from your soul. Do not let the stupidity of some men cause you to question *all* of us. True love *will* find its way to your doorstep. And, when it does, all of the pain you have ever experienced will fade away. Believe it!

Meagan Good: You are too good to go bad, so keep love on your mind and in your heart. If you do that, your earthly experience will be enhanced *tenfold*. I will keep you in my thoughts and prayers. You are more beautiful inside than out!

Sharon Briggs: You are the quintessential example of a woman who is dedicated to spreading Beautiful Black Love to everyone you encounter. Clarence would be so *proud* of you! Keep caring and sharing. It is truly an honor to call you my friend!

All of Malcolm X's Daughters: You have inherited the strength of both your mother and father, so you deserve the same Beautiful Black Love they shared with each other. I have *all* of you close to my heart.

Every Black Woman I Have Ever Hurt: Forgive me for being stupid. I deserve all of the misfortune that came my way as a result of me hurting you. Do not allow my past actions to cause you to mess over your man. He is not the man I once was. If ever I see you again, I will embrace you with nothing but love—if you allow me to.

Every Black Man who has Transcended Black Male Stupidity: The road to wisdom has been a long one, especially for those of us who have had to acquire wisdom on our own. Cherish your Beautiful Black Woman. She needs you, and you need her. Only when the two of you unite in love will mountains be moved.

All of my Haters: For being the fuel that adds velocity to the vehicle I am driving toward success. I appreciate all of the inspiration. I could *never* fail in your presence. Thanks for being an integral part of my life experience, as well as an essential part of my drive and determination. I see you today but will forget you tomorrow!

April Freeman: For believing in me, supporting me, and staying true and real since *day one*. It is because of you that you have this published book in your hands right now, so I thank you. You are absolutely the most amazing friend! Always know and remember that you will have a loyal friend in me for all eternity. We will take our friendship to the grave and continue to enjoy it in the afterlife. Believe it!

Author's Note

Although I have written this book primarily for Black Women, it is also for Black Men. Weak Black Men will view it as a slight to their characters, but those who are strong will understand that this work is *nothing* of the sort. All I have to say about this is, "It is what it is." In addition, some readers may misinterpret the title and assume that I believe all Black Men are stupid. Others may assume that I oppose interracial relationships. Both of these assumptions are false. Like all men, when it comes to male-female relationships, many Black Men do stupid things. And love is not confined by race. However, I *do* believe that there is something special and otherwordly about true love shared by Black couples. Hence, the title. But this book's contents are open to all. If you truly want to understand exactly what this book is about, read the section entitled "Foretroduction: A Foreword and Introduction" before delving into the following chapters. Enjoy!

Throughout this book, in example anecdotes, the real names of all persons mentioned have been changed to protect the true identities of the people upon which said anecdotes are based. Any resemblance to other persons is thus purely coincidental.

Additional Note: Throughout this work, you will notice the capitalization of the first letter in words that do not usually begin with capitalized letters. You will also notice the repetition of certain acronyms. These letters are capitalized because such capitalization is a representation of cultural pride in the African-American community, and acronym repetition is an integral part of this book's overall message. The author urges the reader to memorize the following three terms and their acronyms: Stupid Black Man or Stupid Black Men (SBM), Beautiful Black Love (BBL), and Black Male Stupidity (BMS). And the five primary words or terms that are indicative of cultural pride are "Black," "Black Man," "Black Woman," "Beautiful Black Man," and "Beautiful Black Woman."

Foretroduction

A Foreword and Introduction

When I look back at my life from my current vantage point, I tend to regard my old self with shameful nods. In my youth, I was so *stupid* in the world of relationships! At that time, in my mind, to cherish a woman was to be "weak." So I followed the popular trend and became a "player." Little did I know that the only person I ended up playing was I. Eventually, all of the "games" came back to haunt me. And, for many years afterward, my relationships did not last. I was a Stupid Black Man who knew absolutely *nothing* about Beautiful Black Love (BBL) and my Beautiful Black Women—and then things changed.

In 2002, due to my then rebellious lifestyle and association with certain others, I was incarcerated for armed robbery. In October of that year, in the city of New Orleans, Louisiana, I was convicted and sentenced to 15 years of hard labor, without the possibility of probation or parole. One by one, after hearing that I would have to do at least eighty-five percent of my sentence before seeing the streets again, the women I were with at the time began walking out of my life. Therefore, there I was, lonely, in a cell—just me, myself, and I. All of my so-called comrades also jumped ship on me. The same was true regarding many members of my family. I was bitter and angry and did most of my time on lockdown for causing trouble. In 2003, I was transferred upstate to another prison, where I eventually ended up on lockdown again. And, a few years later, just when I was about to give in to my inner beast and say, "Fuck everything and everybody," God sent a Beautiful Black Woman into my life to get my mind right. This woman was Shandreka—my beautiful big sister.

Shan and I had not talked in quite some time. Before my incarceration, while I was out roaming the streets, she was out traversing the University of New Orleans' college campus, focusing on her future. While I was rotting in a cell, she was making a life for herself. She was highly enthusiastic, focused, happy, and in love. Instead of rejecting me, she wrote to me out of the blue and embraced me with nothing but love and affection, which felt so *good* to me. Her love made me reconsider *everything* I believed. We must have written each other a million letters. She would always stop by the prison to visit me (even after she moved to Georgia) when her hubby and her were in town. And, because we look so much alike, every time I looked at her, I would see myself sitting in front of me. I wanted to be like her. I wanted to have that enthusiasm, that focus, that happiness, that *love*. And that is when I made a conscious decision to follow in the footsteps of a Beautiful Black Woman.

Shortly after this, I stopped getting into trouble, got out of lockdown and, in 2007, was transferred to another prison, where I began to educate myself and take advantage of all the positive opportunities provided to me. I enrolled in school a few days after my arrival at this new penal complex. Four and a half months later, after passing the GED test, I was awarded a General Equivalency Diploma. Then I enrolled in a nearby, accredited community college by way of a grant-backed college program at the prison. I later graduated with an Associate degree in General Studies with a concentration in General Business. And, while I was excelling in college, I was tutoring prisoners in a special education class; mastering American Sign Language and Spanish; excelling at public speaking as a member of the Jaycees organization; reading voraciously on my job as a librarian; writing for the prison magazine; and having my journalism recognized on the front and inner pages of local and national newspapers—all of this and more while incarcerated. I could have gotten full of myself and took all the credit for these accomplishments, but I did not. How could I? Never once did I forget that it was all influenced by the Beautiful Black Love of a Beautiful Black Woman who I am *proud* to call my big sister!

But I said all of that to say this: It is now 2012 and, thanks to my sister, my perception of Black Women—in fact, *all* women—is totally different and where it is supposed to be in regards to inner, as opposed to simply outer, beauty. I admire, respect, and cherish those of the opposite sex, especially my Beautiful Black Queens. They go through sooo much in this male-dominated, chauvinistic world. Yet, they persist, and I love them to death. I love their strength, their compassion, and everything about them, the good *and* the bad. So, when I see Black Men taking their love for granted, it hurts me deep. And this is what inspired me to write this book.

It seems as if everywhere I turn, I see what I call BMS—Black Male Stupidity. I can give BMS a definition but, since action speaks louder than words, I would rather highlight some of these men's actions, which would undoubtedly draw attention to the inanity here referenced. Though there are many examples of such idiocy, I believe that Stupid Black Men can best be characterized by way of the following nine examples.

Nine Examples of Stupid Black Men

1. Those who deliberately cheat on their faithful Black partners.
2. Those who physically and/or mentally abuse Black Women.
3. Those who manipulate and take advantage of Black Women's minds and emotions to get between their thighs.
4. Those who are parasitic and make a living by living off Black Women, using them for financial support.

5. Those whose actions and behaviors are influenced by jealousy because their Black Women are, or are becoming, more financially successful than they are.

6. Those who abandon the Black Women who gave birth to their Beautiful Black children.

7. Those who believe that Black Women are inferior because their physical features do not meet the standards of European-American beauty.

8. Those who turn Black Women into criminals, drug addicts, and/or prostitutes.

9. Those who, without any real interest in interracial relationships, neglect their Black Women for non-Black women—just for the hell of it.

All of these examples are driven by stupidity. I know this because, in the past, I used to fit the description of all but example six. In fact, had I had children back then, the sixth example would have characterized me as well. So I know from *personal* experience how stupid a man can be. In the world of Black relationships, the only *real* cure for BMS is Beautiful Black Love, which I also believe cannot be comprehended by definition alone. Therefore, in order to paint a clear picture of what I consider Beautiful Black Love, I would rather use real-life, Black marital relationships as examples. There are many such relationships to which I can turn but, off the top of my brain, only five come to mind.

Five Beautiful Black Love Marital Relationships

1. Coretta Scott and Martin Luther King's marriage.
2. Betty and Malcolm Shabazz's marital relationship.
3. Michelle and Barack Obama's marital union.
4. Jada Pinkett and Will Smith's matrimony.
5. Serita and T.D. Jakes' marriage.

When one looks at the love shared between the partners involved in each of these Black relationships, it is easy to see what I mean regarding such love being beautiful. And this is the kind of love that Black Men need to share with their Beautiful Black Women.

I see so many single Black women out there in society, and other Black Women who are stuck in relationships that are void of BBL, and I wish that I could be the one to give them the Beautiful Black Love that they deserve. In the world of Black celebrity, my heart goes out to successful Black Women like Kandi Burruss, Zoe Saldana, and Sanaa Lathan, whose hearts are not, at the time of this writing (according to the media), caught up in the rapture of Beautiful Black Love. I can see myself happily growing old with any one of them. The same is true regarding the Beautiful Black Women I recently read about in the October 2011 issue of *Ebony* magazine, in Audra D.S. Burch's article about sexy singles.

I also look at old couples who are celebrating 50-plus years of matrimony, and I become saddened by the fact that so many Black Women are not experiencing this kind of long-lasting love. After pondering this for quite some time, I have come to the conclusion that, oftentimes, the problem is not them—the problem is usually the result of Black Male Stupidity. Stupid Black Men need to wake up! And this is what I am talking about in this book.

Below is a concise book and chapter outline, should you decide to read on beyond these first opening pages.

Concise Book and Chapter Outline

This book is divided into two parts. There is Part One, Stupid Black men, and Part Two, Beautiful Black Love. The former consists of nine chapters, each of which elaborates on one of the aforementioned examples of Black Male Stupidity. In this part, I also discuss the problems caused by the BMS highlighted in each chapter. In the latter part, however, I discuss all of the following: (1) the primary lessons that Black Men can learn from the BBL couples mentioned above; (2) the benefits of BBL acceptance; (3) the loving nature of the Black Woman; and (4) what I believe will happen if Stupid Black Men remain stupid. Then, at the end of the book, I include a personal love letter/lyric poem from me to all the Beautiful Black Women out there in the world. Beautiful Black Woman, you are MINE! You belong to ME! So you better read my love letter!

Anyway, if you, the reader, are a Black Woman, and you believe that you are worthy of Beautiful Black Love, then, for you, this book is a must read. If you are a Black Man who are or once was characterized by any of the above Black Male Stupidity examples, then you should read this book, too. In fact, *all* Black Men and Women should read it. In addition, if you are just a curious reader who, for whatever reason(s), are interested in the subject of Beautiful Black Love, then feel free to read on. African, Hispanic, Asian, European, whatever—all are welcome, as long as you have good, honest intentions. If we all work together to spread Beautiful Black Love across the globe, the world will truly be a better place.

Whoever you are, I hope this book inspires you. If it does and you would like to contact me, you can do so by way of the information listed on the Contact the Author page at the back of this book. I prefer handwritten letters over all other forms of communication but will be happy to hear from you regardless of whichever means you choose. And I will try my best to respond to your mail in a timely manner.

Despite however things may seem, Beautiful Black Love is not dead in this world. It is just repressed. Yet, it is yearning to burst out of the cages that so many of us Black people have

PART 1

STUPID BLACK MEN

Chapter One
Unfaithfulness and Betrayal

Infidelity. Disloyalty. Adultery. Unfaithfulness. Betrayal. In the world of Black relationships, it seems as if all of these words describe the actions executed by a great number of Black American men. Whether these actions are influenced by popular culture or passed down from one generation to the next, or both, is arguable. However, the origin or cause of such actions, though important, is not more important than the need to modify the beliefs that *fuel* these actions. So, in order to effect positive change in the world of Black relationships, it is imperative that we discuss both belief origin *and* belief modification. The solution to our problem lies in the proper alteration of misguided ideology, not just in acquired knowledge about misguided ideology's beginnings. Therefore, on the subject of unfaithfulness and betrayal, this chapter explores one aspect of the misguided ideology that leads to the stupid behavior carried out by Black Men involved in Black relationships. So, too, do the following eight chapters. But the belief modification aspect of this discussion will be addressed in Chapter 10. In this *first* chapter, however, let us elaborate on the stupidity of unfaithfulness and betrayal, and the problems these things cause regarding Black relationships.

One thing I must note before moving on is that what is generally accepted is not always true. Popular opinion says that, in order to find a solution to a problem, one must first find its cause or origin. However, I beg to differ. When firefighters are called to a burning building, they put the fire out first and *then* begin investigating the fire's origin. When a reckless driver is on the run from policemen, the policemen's primary objective is putting an end to the reckless driver's getaway. Once the driver is stopped, discovering the exact cause or origin of his getaway attempt is usually the *secondary* objective. These simple examples prove that a problem can be solved without primary focus upon a problem's origin. So, if unfaithfulness and betrayal in Black relationships is a problem, and indeed it is, then we should focus on stopping the problem instead of worrying only about where it all started. With that said, let us move on.

Misguided Ideology

In general, in America, when it comes to misguided ideology, as much as I hate to say this, Black Men's ideology is atop of the list of that which is most misguided. This does not apply to *all* Black Men, of course. But an honest person cannot deny the fact the large numbers of Black Men do some really stupid things—especially to their Beautiful Black Women. They are the ones who the late author Carter G. Woodson would no doubt label "miseducated." Such Black Men are found wherever there are Black Men. And, the younger they are, it seems, the stupider they are. To show you what I mean, here are two accounts of my encounters with such men.

Approximately two weeks ago, while I was preparing to take a test for American Sign Language interpreting, I met a 20-year-old, African-American man who, after seeing me signing with a friend, approached me and claimed to have a sincere interest in learning American Sign Language. This turned into a somewhat lengthy conversation about the Deaf community. He asked many questions about Deaf culture. He wanted to know what motivated me to learn how to sign. And, just when I was beginning to believe that I had a new, sincere, potentially serious the Washington Monument with a lengthy shoestring in place of a bungee cord, she would probably fall to sudden death beside him—and enjoy it. Yes, I believe that she loves him just this much. And I *swear* I am not exaggerating. Well, anyway, this man, I later discovered, cheated on his wife dozens of times with a woman half his age. He claims he was addicted to Viagra, which he believes made him cheat.

The first man cheated on his wife because the two of them had not had sex in a while, and he was too weak to maintain his composure in the presence of a distraught, attractive woman. The second man gave in to his lust for younger women and ended up cheating on his spouse. Judging from this and what I personally know about these men, I can reasonably state that their ideologies were, frankly, fucked up. The first man believed that it is okay to cheat on a woman if she steers clear of sex for a while. The second man believed that, if a wife is overly supportive, then a husband can cheat on her and get away with it. Both of these men are stupid. Their viewpoints are distorted. They, like the two younger Black Men mentioned prior, are prime examples of Black Men with misguided ideologies. And their unfaithfulness is more than just unfaithfulness—it is utter betrayal. In the world of Black relationships, the worst thing Black Men can do is betray their Beautiful Black Women. Yet, great numbers of our women (when I say "great numbers," I mean *millions*) have been betrayed by our actions, disgraced, and dishonored by our stupidity. This causes a great deal of problems.

Problems Caused by Unfaithfulness and Betrayal

After studying a large number of relationships that have been affected—and sometimes utterly destroyed—by infidelity, I have concluded that infidelity in relationships causes five primary problems. These problems are:

1. Loss of trust.
2. Complication of forgiveness.
3. Worsening of existing problems.
4. Setting of bad examples for children.
5. Potential destruction of the scorned partner's future relationships.

By no means do these five problems encompass all of the problems caused by unfaithfulness and betrayal. However, I believe that any other problems caused by infidelity can be considered sub-problems of those that are listed above. Now, let us elaborate on these problems.

Loss of Trust

Oftentimes, because women are such fragile creatures, despite how "hard" some may seem on the surface, it takes a lot for them to trust a man. This is particularly true regarding most Black Women. Such women study the men they are involved with, learn everything they need to know about them before they open their hearts to these men. And only when they are convinced that letting down their guards will not get them hurt will they open up and allow themselves to trust these men. And, when things get serious and strong bonds are created, all of the walls surrounding these women's emotions usually come down. This may not mean much to men but, to women, this is a big deal. One wrong move by a man can cause a woman's trust to fade away into the darkness of Never Again Land. Trust that took *years* to build can vanish in *seconds*.

I have talked to many Black Men about this, and many of them, in so many words, said that breaking their women's trust was one of the stupidest things they could have ever done. They said that, after their women found out about their infidelity, they had to go through hell to gain their women's trust again. And this newly earned trust, from what they told me, is not as strong as the trust their women had before. According to one Black Man I talked to, even though his fiancée decided to remain engaged to him after he cheated, her "spider senses go off" every time he is anywhere near another woman. He said that, no matter how much he tries to make things right, she will never again trust him the same way she used to, which causes him to feel perpetually guilty.

This is usually what happens when a Black Man betrays a Black Woman's trust and he and that woman stay together. After his woman's trust factor hits zero, things are *never* the same again. That man is subject to suspicion, even when he is one hundred percent innocent, which is both uncomfortable and stressful, though he brought all of this upon himself. But, most of the time, a Black Woman will not stand for this and will leave his unfaithful ass. And, when this happens, it is oftentimes "bye-bye" to Beautiful Black Love.

Complication of Forgiveness

In life, period, once trust is broken and betrayed, it is oftentimes hard for *any* person hurt by betrayal to forgive the person who has betrayed her or him. In fact, for as long as I can remember, forgiveness has always been one of *my* greatest struggles. So, in many ways, I understand how hard it is for betrayed women to forgive their betrayers. When it comes to relationships, especially those in the Black world, complication of forgiveness that is caused by infidelity throws relationships off balance. And, if a relationship is not balanced, it falls victim to its unbalanced aspects. Here are two examples of unbalanced relationships that unfaithfulness has rendered unstable.

Lynn and Brian have been together for seven and a half years. At the beginning of their relationship, Lynn, who has been hurt before, tells Brian not to break her heart, to be a real man who does not play childish games with people's emotions. Brian promises to be the real man he is always claiming to be. He says he will never cheat on her. But, five years into the relationship, Brian and Lynn begin having some problems that lead to frequent arguments. After one particularly heated argument, they break up for a while and eventually get back together. But Lynn discovers that Brian had sex with one of her so-called friends during the temporary breakup, and Brian is denying that this ever happened. So Lynn's trust factor hits zero. Brian then confesses to cheating, apologizes, says he loves her and wants to start over, and Lynn gives him another chance. But she finds it difficult to forgive him completely. She makes constant reference to his unfaithfulness, rubs it in his face every time they argue about something, even though Brian is completely faithful now. He begs for her forgiveness, but she just cannot find the strength to forgive and forget. So, now they are about to break up again—for good. Who is to blame? Some people would say Lynn, because she will not forgive Brian. But, in reality, Brian is to blame because, during a temporary breakup, he made a stupid, traitorous move.

In another example, Wilbert and Shanel just got married and are fresh off their honeymoon. In Shanel's mind, she is living her dream with the man of her dreams. In Wilbert's mind, Shanel was made for him, and they will ride or die together in love until the end. They are financially stable, have big dreams, and the future seems promising. But, as the years go by, Wilbert realizes that, according to his own ideology, the married life is "not all it is cracked up to be." He finds himself fussing with Shanel about what he believes to be stupid things, but things that are obviously important to her. And sex with her is not the same. To him, this whole "marriage and sex thing" is boring, and he is growing tired of waking up to the same woman with the same problems every day. He yearns to cut loose from the confines of marriage. He wants to be entertained. So, after explaining all of this to one of his bachelor friends, he decides to go out with the "fellas" and have a night on the town.

He and his friends go first to a strip club and then to a concert at the local House of Blues. At the strip club, as he receives a lap dance from a hottie, he reminisces about old times he shared with Shanel, when she would dance and strip for him in the privacy of their own home. But this pisses him off, because it also reminds him of how much Shanel has changed during their marriage. So he and his friends leave. Afterwards, at the concert, another hottie approaches him and requests a dance. As their bodies become one on the dance floor, he is reminded of Shanel again, the way that he and she used to dance. Anyway, he ends up kissing this woman, one thing lead to another, and they have sex all night at a nearby hotel. He does not make it home until the next morning.

Waiting on him for hours, Shanel inquires about where he was and "what he was doing last night," which turns into a heated argument. Pissed, Wilbert admits that he cheated and blames it on her. She then packs her things and leaves. After a two-month separation, they agree to get back together, so she moves back in. He feels guilty about cheating, but she says it is all "old news," not to worry about it. Then *she* begins cheating behind *his* back, and *he* finds out. After a heated argument, *he* packs *his* things and leaves. She leaves a message on his voicemail stating that revenge is sweet and she cheated because he broke her heart, destroyed her trust, and she will never forgive him.

Who is the blame attributed to in this example? Although she could have handled the situation a lot better, I believe Shanel's actions do not make her the bearer of blame. She was simply lashing out emotionally because Wilbert betrayed her by doing what he did. Thus, it is his fault—not hers.

In both of these example relationships, unforgiveness is caused by unfaithfulness and betrayal executed by Stupid Black Men. We all know that having sex with one of our girlfriend's friends is very uncool, even during temporary or any other kinds of breakups. In addition, we also know that temporary breakups are not really considered *true* breakups, which are permanent. Therefore, if a person has sex with another person during a temporary breakup, it is still infidelity. When women like Lynn and Shanel are driven into unforgiveness by the foolish actions of men like Brian and Wilbert, this drastically weakens the power of Beautiful Black Love.

Worsening of Existent Problems

Of course, no relationship, marital or otherwise, is perfect. But what makes a relationship great is when loving partners can resolve their problems in reasonable ways. This is not as easy as it seems, though, which explains why so many people in relationships find themselves arguing constantly about all kinds of things, why they have so many problems. During all of this chaos, especially if the partners are trying really hard to get things right, stupid behavior carried out by one or both of the partners only worsens the existent problems. And, when such stupid behavior manifests by way of infidelity, all hell breaks loose. The arguments get worse. Trust issues grow more intense. Stress levels reach an all-time high. Hearts get broken again. The list goes on and on. This is why so many relationships do not last long enough to stand the test of time, which is a serious problem. How can Beautiful Black Love survive if problems are always getting worse, if one is always cheating on the person he claims to love? Continuous fussing and fighting will not get partners anywhere meaningful, does not benefit a relationship. Infidelity utterly destroys attempts at reconciliation. Betrayal is a big slap in the face to love itself. So, if Black Men really want to keep their Beautiful Black Women, they need to keep their dicks in their pants. When they fail to do so, their stupidity only exacerbates their problems.

Setting of Bad Examples for Children

When I was growing up, many of the older women I knew were in relationships with men who cheated on them regularly. Most of my friends' mothers were prime examples of this. Although, oftentimes, these women were cognizant of their mates' infidelity, they never ever said a word about it. They just pretended everything was all fine and dandy, when in reality they were very heartbroken. Some of these women stayed with their men because they needed the financial stability the men provided. Others were just hoping that their men would change their unfaithful ways, even though they knew better. I saw all of this with my own eyes, but I could not speak out about it because, in their minds, I was "just a child." So, whenever these men would come around me, or I would spend time around them, I would just watch them do to their women whatever it was they wanted to do to them. As I grew older, after watching such men for so long, I began thinking, "I want to be *just* like them." I really looked up to them. They were my role models, whether they knew this or not. For both their own children and me, they set bad examples—really bad examples.

I see so much of the same thing going on nowadays when I peer out into the world. On television, in books and magazines, and throughout *all* American communities, countless men glorify infidelity. And countless children who look up to them are glorifying what they glorify, so much so that this problem has gotten outrageously out of hand, and some of these children will tell an adult face-to-face that infidelity is cool. For instance, about two years ago, one of my associates asked his 15-year-old daughter the following question: "Instead of running behind all these boys, why don't you think about saving yourself for marriage?" His daughter responded, "Because Momma didn't save herself for you, and you didn't save yourself for Momma. Plus, you cheated on her *beaucoup* times." He then asked her how she would feel if a boy cheated on *her* like that. And, to this, she responded, "I wouldn't care as long as he really loves me. Besides, it's *natural* for boys to mess around these days." "Natural?" he asked, to no one in particular. Then his face dropped. But it was all *his* fault. Why? Because, as an unfaithful Black Man, he had set bad examples for his own child, as well as many other children.

This is just one of the many things that happens when parents cheat. And, because so many Black Men seem to cheat just for fun, many Black children, especially Black boys, usually end up following in their fathers' adulterous footsteps. No sane man should want this for his child or children. Black fathers really need to think about this before they yield to their libidos and engage in stupid, adulterous behavior.

Potential Destruction of a Scorned Partner's Future Relationships

Several years ago, I met and became emotionally involved with an older woman who was severely scorned by Black Men.

Let us call her Gwenn. About a month after I posted an ad on a particular website, I received a letter from Gwenn, who was about 12 years older than I. After reading my ad and falling in love with my photo, Gwenn said that she wanted to "get to know me on a personal level and see where things will lead." I wrote her back, and we just hit it off. Things were going really nice between us. When I kissed her for the first time, oooh it was heaven—then all of my joy became hell. Gwenn started "tripping," just went all crazy on me. "Are you seeing somebody else? I *know* that you are." "I know you're after my money." "I know you're plotting to leave me and, if you do, I'm going to track you down and cut your big dick off!" These are just *some* of the things she told me (no emphasis added). She started accusing me of stuff I had never done. She was overly suspicious. We were always fussing. So, I just called it quits, cut her off without warning. Well, about six months later, I decided to check up on her and see if she was okay, so I wrote her a letter. She wrote me back apologizing and explained everything. I conducted a little investigation into what she told me and discovered that she was telling me the truth.

Gwenn had been raped by her biological father, abandoned by her biological mother, and physically abused by four different Black Men, all of whom were incarcerated at the time that she explained all of this. In addition, her father had cheated on her mother, her mother had cheated on her father, and all four of the men who battered her cheated on her as well. She had some serious issues. Well, anyway, Gwenn and I eventually lost contact, so I do not know where she is now, whether she is even still alive. But I think about her from time to time and, when I do, her life story reminds me that she was and is the product of what those Stupid Black Men made her. And this is why none of her relationships have ever lasted. Since Gwenn, I have seen many other "Gwenns" walking the earth. Because of Stupid Black Men, they all lack Beautiful Black Love.

Now, I know that every woman's relationship situation is different, that each woman's situation is not exactly like Gwenn's. But there are many scorned Black Women out there in the world who cannot maintain a relationship because of what previous Black Men have done to them. And, in most of these situations that were caused by these men, infidelity and betrayal usually have something to do with it. Black Men, pay attention, because this is what you are putting many of your Black Women through when you take their love for granted, play with their hearts and emotions, and cheat on them. You destroy them psychologically, which is stupid.

Misguided ideology is responsible for all of the hurtful things mentioned in this chapter. If the Black Men discussed here would have taken the time to study both themselves and their Black Women, and had they done this simply out of love, their relationships would not have failed. But the fact is that they *did* do what they did, and loss of trust, complication of forgiveness, worsening of existent problems, bad example setting, and destruction of future relationships were the results. In order to prevent this from happening again on a larger scale, Black Men of today need to learn from these problems and avoid making the same mistakes. Unfaithfulness and betrayal are predicated on stupidity. It destroys relationships, but love conquers all. Therefore, my beloved Black Brothers, if you truly love your Beautiful Black Women, do not fall victim to misguided ideology. By cherishing and remaining true to them, you will experience BBL and bask in joy and happiness for all the rest of your days.

Chapter Two
Physical and Mental Abusers

In the United States of America, domestic violence is, in many ways, similar to a plague. Women are battered daily, in nearly every neighborhood, in every state. In fact, according to *The Advocate,* a new survey shows that 1 in every 4 American women is and/or has been battered in some way at least once in her life. But what is even more shocking is that such women number in the millions. I recently stumbled upon these findings while perusing the latest issue of the *Walk Talk* magazine, which mentions the survey. "As many as 29 million women say they have suffered severe violence from a boyfriend, spouse or other intimate partner, including reports of being beaten, stabbed, shot, punched, slammed, or had their hair pulled. That number increases to 36 million when slapping and shoving are added to the list," the *Walk Talk* says. These are some startling statistics regarding domestic violence. After discovering this, I did some further research on this matter and found out that, several years ago, a Department of Justice report revealed that lower income women are more likely to be abused by their partners. This Department of Justice report is referenced in Richard J. Gelles' article entitled "Domestic Violence," which appears in *Encarta Reference Library Premium 2005.* "The DOJ report indicated that intimate violence occurs almost equally among women of all races and slightly more likely to occur among women with low incomes," Gelles writes. Well, we Americans are very well aware that the term "low income," though it *can* mean women of *all* races, *usually* means "African-American." Therefore, according to the DOJ report, most domestic abuse victims are Black females.

Of course, as an African-American man who grew up in the slums in the South, I have seen the horror of domestic violence with my own eyes. So I do not have to read a report to know what many of my Beautiful Black Women have experienced and are still experiencing at the hands of their abusers. I simply quoted the aforementioned statistics and mentioned the DOJ report because backing assertions with publicly known and documented fact is standard practice for writers. But I do not believe that statistics and surveys, no matter how in depth they are, can accurately reveal the severity of domestic abuse in Black America. This compels one to ask, "What exactly is the cause of domestic violence in Black communities?" There are many different answers, but I believe that all of these answers point to the same thing: Black Male Stupidity. This is because only a Stupid Black Man would batter a Beautiful Black Woman.

Prior to writing this book, I conducted dozens of my own surveys, on a wide range of topics, primarily those pertinent to this book. And, during my domestic violence-related survey, I talked to many Black Men who have abused women in the past, and even some who told me that they will *never* change, because they believe that they are woman beaters by nature. I want to take you into the minds of some of these men so that you can see just how ridiculous their beliefs are. First, I will discuss Charles and Timothy, both of whom were reared in suburban neighborhoods by well-to-do parents. Discussion regarding Tyler and Jamie, who grew up in middle-class neighborhoods, will follow. Then you will meet Teddy and Gavin, two Black Men from the ghetto. Though they all grew up in different environments, their beliefs make them all essentially the same—stupid.

Charles

Charles grew up in Atlanta, Georgia. His mother holds a respectable position at a bank, and his father is CEO of a successful, international business. From birth until his college graduation, Charles resided in an affluent gated community with his parents, a place where crime was and still is nearly nonexistent. After college, Charles moved out on his own and entered the dating scene as a bachelor. Two years later, after impregnating one of his lovers, he decided to settle down with this soon-to-be mother of his child. He wanted to be a great father. But, after the baby was born, things changed. He found himself constantly depressed. He began to hate the presence of his child's mother, whom he believed "trapped him into marriage." Then he just snapped.

After returning home from work one day, his wife bombarded him with all kinds of complaints regarding his share of the responsibility concerning the child. And, as she stood there in front of him "yapping off at the mouth," he reached out and put both of his hands around her neck, forcibly pushed her against a nearby wall, and choked her hard until she passed out, at which point he then released his grip and allowed her limp body to fall to the floor with a loud thump. The next morning, she went to him crying and apologizing for the way she had approached him the previous day. He accepted her apology and then apologized to her for what he had done. Then they made love. But, just one month later, he was choking her again. And the choking was followed by slaps to her face. He went on to batter her regularly for three years—until she took their child and left him. Now they are divorced and he can only spend time with his child on weekends.

Well, I asked Charles, "Initially, why did you choke your wife? And why did you choke her until she passed out?" This is what he told me: "Honestly, man, I don't even know. I guess I kind of blacked out or whatever. I was exhausted and tired of her running her big mouth, so I guess the only way to shut her up was to choke her good until she fell out. Sometimes a man needs peace and quiet." "What's peaceful about choking the woman you claim to love until she passes out?" I asked him. He did not respond. I told him to his face that his reason for hurting his wife in such a way was barbaric, unmanly, and flat out stupid. And, before our discussion ended, he admitted to me that he was ashamed of his stupidity. He also said that his father never abused his mother, so he cannot explain what truly urged him to do such a thing.

Timothy

Like Charles, Timothy also grew up in a gated suburban community with his well-off parents. But, unlike Charles, Timothy's parents, who were civil rights activists during the Martin Luther King Jr. era, were always fussing and fighting behind closed doors, while portraying an image of marital bliss when out in public. And, on several occasions, Timothy witnessed his father punching his mother in the face. When I talked to Timothy, however, he insisted that he is his own man, makes his own decisions, so his parents relationship has nothing to do with him battering his own wife. I disagreed, of course. But, for the sake of respecting his wishes, let us assume that Timothy's father's abusive actions have had no influence upon Timothy.

Moving on now, here is what happened with Timothy. He has been married twice, the first time to a woman he fell in love with in college; the second time to a woman he met while on vacation in Jamaica. His first marriage ended because he and his wife just grew apart. They are still friends, however. His second marriage ended because he beat his wife so much that he broke her jaw, and she pressed charges against him. He only did a few months in prison. They are now divorced and reside in different states. I asked him why he broke his wife's jaw and this was his response: "I don't care what other people say or think but, if I'm in a married relationship with a woman, and she is one of those feminist types who is hell bent on not submitting to me, then it is my duty as a man to make her submit. If that requires me to physically put her in check, then so be it. I have no regrets."

Obviously, Timothy is a male chauvinist. But his biggest problem is that he has serious control issues. He seems to have adopted the old European-American belief that women are totally inferior to men. I told him that this is 21st century America, where both women and men are equal, despite any and/or all attempts to convince the world otherwise. His response to this was, "America, no matter *what* century it is, is and will always be a predominantly Christian nation. I am a Christian, and in Christianity the woman is taught to submit. So I will make her submit." We debated this for a while, then our discussion ended. Timothy sincerely believes that he did not truly batter his wife. In his opinion, he simply adhered to Christian principles by putting her in her place—physically. This way of thinking is what makes him stupid.

Tyler

Like me, Tyler grew up in the city of New Orleans, Louisiana, but in a different neighborhood, in a different social class. His neighborhood was middle-class. His mother and father divorced when he was a teenager, but both have been very active in his life. According to Tyler, there was no evidence of spousal abuse in his parents' relationship prior to divorce. Thus, from what he himself has told me, he cannot understand how or why he turned out to be an abuser of women. He even said that he adored females in his youth. He also said that none of his siblings have ever been in abusive relationships so, to him, what he has become is a mystery.

Anyway, Tyler got married to his high school sweetheart one year after their high school graduation. He thought they would be together forever—he was wrong. One day he encountered an old female friend at a convenience store, and they exchanged cell phone numbers. Before he could tell his wife about the encounter, she found the number while snooping through his cell phone. They got into an argument, she accused him of infidelity, threatened to leave him, and he "just couldn't take this crap anymore." So he grabbed his wife by her hair, punched her in the face, and then threw her down to the floor. He said her fear of him gave him a newfound power over her, so he "started punching her just for fun" on a daily basis. Then, about eight months later, she fled to another state and divorced him.

Although Tyler says that he does not know exactly what would ever make him beat a woman, one particular statement he made revealed his overwhelming stupidity. "Since there isn't really any history of domestic violence in my family, I am led to believe that maybe it is human nature for a man to want to attack his woman. Maybe this urge is man's payback for what Eve did to Adam." After hearing this, I stared at Tyler blank-faced. Mentally, he was so far gone that he was absolutely unaware of his own stupidity.

Jamie

Jamie grew up in a middle-class neighborhood in New York. He has two brothers and four sisters. His parents have been married since before his birth, and they have no history of domestic violence. One of his older sisters, however, has always "seemed to end up with guys who like hitting women." He once befriended one of his sister's abusive boyfriends, and several months later he ended up "putting his fists to the faces of almost every chic he dated." He told me that his life story proves that all women, despite how much they may deny it, *like* to get punched in the face. "Just think about it," he said. "Women do all kinds of stupid shit just to start a fuss and make a man angry. And, after you hit them, most of them do things that are stupider than the last thing they did. In subtle ways, they *ask* to be punched in the face." When we talked about this, Tyler was convinced that all of his assertions were true. My final words to him were, "When you end up in prison for battery of some sort, seriously ponder whose actions were the stupidest—yours or the woman's."

Teddy and Gavin

I have encountered quite a number of Stupid Black Men in my lifetime but, in all honesty, I believe that Teddy and Gavin are undoubtedly among the stupidest. I will discuss them together, because they are very alike and maintain many of the same beliefs regarding Black Women. Teddy is from upstate New York, and Gavin is from uptown New Orleans. The former considers himself a "northern playboy"; the latter, a "gangsta who knows bitches like the back of his hand." Both said that they are "hood" and they will remain the same until death. And they both believe that battering women just comes with the territory, so to speak, in the world of relationships. They put the "S" in "SBM." To show you what I mean, here are a few quotes from each of them.

> Teddy: "A bitch knows her place in my world. But if she falls *out* of place, after I beat the bitch, she'll fall back in line." "These whores out here need *discipline*, and I'm a *god*. If they disrespect God, my fists will give'em hell." "I'll kick *any* bitch into submission if I have to."

> Gavin: "Dawg, I don't give a fuck! A ho is a ho, and a man is a man. So, if a ho don't respect that man, that man needs to *deal* with that ho . . . punch her fucking *lights* out." "I ain't gon' lie to you, homie. I beat bitches *all* the time, and they *love* it. And then I fuck'em like ninety going west." "A gangsta ain't gon' let no ho talk to him stupid. If he does, then he's just as much of a ho as she is, and *both* of 'em need to be slapped."

See what I mean? Teddy and Gavin are Stupid Black Men who prefer Black Male Stupidity over Beautiful Black Love. Males like these perpetuate BMS to the detriment of BBL. And other males like Charles, Timothy, Tyler, and Jamie only make things worse for our Beautiful Black Women. Thus far, I have elaborated only on physical abuse. Here is what a few other Stupid Black Men had to say regarding mental abuse.

> Johnny: "What women call 'mental abuse' is not really mental abuse to me. I think women just get mad when you tell them the truth. My fiancée is fat and stupid, and I tell her that all the time. The truth is the truth. How is that mental abuse?"

Darren: "Women are always blowing shit out of proportion. She does something dumb, you tell her what she did was dumb, and she starts crying. How in the hell is that mental abuse? I'm not about to hold my tongue. I'm not weak!"

Tyrone: "My baby momma was the *shit* before she got pregnant and gave birth to my daughter. She used to work out and everything. Now she's fat as hell, like a human blimp. I tell her this every day, many times. I'm not mentally abusing her—I'm just getting her mind right."

Byron: "I'm used to dating and being with dime piece dames, but I was forced to settle down with my girlfriend after I popped a seed in her. She's sweet, but she's ugly. We're always fussing when I tell her she's ugly. *All* ugly chics say they're being mentally abused when you tell them they're ugly."

After talking to these men and many others, I have concluded that, normally, Stupid Black Men are so stupid that they do not even know what true mental abuse is. In their minds, the awful things they tell their women are just truths that should be accepted. However, some of these men know *exactly* what they are doing, are well aware of what mental abuse is, yet deliberately abuse their women psychologically for a variety of reasons.

All of the examples cited in this chapter paint only a small picture of what is going on in Black America regarding the physical and mental abuse of our beloved Black Women. In total reality, the situation is way worse. I know of men who have pushed their pregnant girlfriends down flights of stairs after beating them. I have heard stories of men pouring gasoline on their lovers and setting them on fire after beating them. And, all the time, it seems, I meet women, abuse survivors, with their own horror stories to tell. Stupid Black Men have scarred them for life—literally. From everyday Black Women in our communities to celebrities like Rihanna, who was allegedly brutally beaten by her ex-boyfriend, Chris Brown, in 2009, the horror of domestic violence afflicts our Beautiful Women. This is just one of the many harsh things our women go through. If we Black Men do not get ourselves together soon, all hope for our women will be lost. As for the problems caused by physical and mental abuse, aside from physical injury, these problems are the same as the five primary problems caused by unfaithfulness and betrayal, just more intense. These problems—lost of trust, complication of forgiveness, worsening of existent problems, bad example setting for children, and potential destruction of the scorned partner's future relationships—are listed and elaborated on in Chapter One. Because of the mental abuse discussed in this chapter, low self-esteem can be added to the list. Truly, we are putting our women through hell.

Chapter Three
Mind and Emotion
Manipulators

Across the globe, it is well-known that women are often taken advantage of by men who manipulate their minds and emotions to get what they want. And sex is at the top of the list of things that men want from women. In fact, this is so true that most men are probably guilty of manipulating the mind and emotions of at least one woman at least one time in their lives. Even I myself was once guilty of this. And I see this happening almost everywhere I turn. In my quest to understand why men treat women this way, I perused random psychology books in search of answers. I acquired some helpful information, but it seems as if even psychologists do not really know why we men do what we do to our women. In fact, in many ways, they usually tell us things that we either already know inherently from human experience or can find out easily just by observing ourselves and our surroundings.

For example, in Chapter 11 of Karen Huffman's textbook *Psychology In Action* (Eight Edition), a chart labeled as Table 11.2 and titled "Research-Supported Sex and Gender Differences" reveals, among other things, the followng: (1) Men's sex lives start earlier than women's; (2) men are more likely to initiate both casual and intimate touch with their sexual partners; and (3) men typically have higher self-esteem than women. This information, in essence, only says what most of us already know, that men are usually more sexually active than women, typically make the first affectionate moves, and are generally more confident. But this in no way addresses the "Why?" of the mind and emotion manipulation question. And most psychology books all fail to address the same. Plus, a significant number of such books are written by non-Black authors who have never conducted any in-depth studies in the Black world regarding this subject. Therefore, after failing to find answers to said question, I was compelled to do research of my own. And here is what I discovered.

When it all boils down to it, the cause of female-targeted mind and emotion manipulation in the Black world is lack of Black Woman-related intelligence, perception, and common sense, which drive the extremely rash and thoughtless behavior of so many Black Men. In other words, Black Male Stupidity is to blame.

I have talked to many Black Men about all of this. Some were smart, but many were stupid. Much of what I learned during my discussions with men of the latter type revealed that many of our Black Men are so far gone that they do not know how to *not* manipulate Black Women's minds and emotions in order to get between their thighs. Later on in this chapter, we will discuss the problems caused by this. But, first, let me introduce you to a few of the men I talked to so that you can see and understand how such men think.

Ralph

Ralph is a forty-something bachelor who has no children, has never been married, and plans to remain a bachelor for the rest of his life. He considers himself a "seducer of the most supreme variety," and he has Robert Green's bestselling book *The Art of Seduction* down pat. In fact, he has memorized all of the book's key elements. His demeanor is that of a shrewd and intelligent businessman, but when he starts talking about women, he sounds like he could be a modern-day pimp. This is what he told me at the beginning of our discussion: "I've been a player for a long time now, ever since my great uncle passed the game down to me. And one thing I know about women is that *most* of them *want* to be seduced. Women make men think they are manipulating her mind and emotions, but she is the *true* manipulator. That's why I *never* pass up an opportunity to seduce my way into a woman's thighs." "What if the female's mind is young and underdeveloped, but the male's mind is much older and fully developed?" I asked Ralph, in response. "Can a mind that's underdeveloped manipulate a mature mind into thinking that it, the mature mind, is doing the seducing?" "Yes," he answered. "This is why we see so many older guys being the lovers of younger women. These older men are manipulated into believing that they are manipulating their way into the younger women's vaginas. But these younger women wanted the older men the whole time."

After discussing this for a while, I asked Ralph how many young women had he slept with in the past year or so, and whether he felt guilty at any time about having sex with them and telling them whatever it is he told them in order to have sex with them. After mentally calculating the number of young sex partners he had had, he admitted that, without his cell phone nearby, he could not give me an exact number. "But I estimate that it's somewhere between 60 and 70," he said. "And, no, I don't feel, and have never felt, guilty about my dealings with them. I told them what they wanted to hear, got them emotionally involved, and we did our thing—and they all liked it." The youngest female he has ever slept with was 17. He was in his thirties when he met her. He also said that, after their first sexual encounter, this young female fell madly in love with him, and he waited until she was 18 to break her heart and get rid of her. I told him that, according to all the stuff he told me, if this young female was so shrewd at seducing him to have sex with her, and sex was all she wanted, then she would not have allowed herself to get so emotionally attached. He disagreed and said that she wanted all of that all the while. I could not change his mind. I told him that, legally, in certain states, he would be considered a pedophile that preys on weak-minded, young Black girls. He got mad. The discussion ended.

In many ways, many Black Men in America are just like Ralph. They may not seek out as many young sex partners as he did, but they do believe that they are justified in what they say and do to manipulate the minds and emotions of young Black Women in order to have sex with them.

Kendall

As far as age and female preference goes, Kendall is the opposite of Ralph. He is 29 years of age and preys on *older* women, particularly those who are widows or married but discontent with marriage and their husbands. Kendall puts it this way: "I love turning older, non-cougar women into cougars. It's a like a game, the way I have to manipulate their resistant minds and play with their emotions just to get them into bed. If she's already a cougar, that takes the fun out of it, because I want to be the one to break her in." Kendall is a bachelor. However, he has one child, a 10-yr-old daughter. Her mother is 15 years Kendall's senior. She was the first older woman he "broke," but their relationship did not work because she "tried to rope him into marriage," and he "wasn't feeling that." So they split, and he has been dating older women ever since.

I asked Kendall what kind of pleasure does he normally get out of manipulating the minds and emotions of such women, and this was his response: "It gives me power knowing that, with my gift of gab alone, I can control the minds of women older than me, that I can bring the freak out of them and make them do things they never thought they would do." But what really shocked me was what he said when I asked him how he would feel if some other young guy were to take advantage of his mother like that. "Honestly, I wouldn't care, because my mother is a grown woman who makes her own decisions. Who am I to judge? Plus, if I like the dude, after my mother and him fade out or whatever, we could hook up. He could be my cougar-making partner."

I know a lot of men like Kendall. Some of them would probably disagree with the assertion he made regarding his mother, but others would definitely share the same belief. My personal opinion is that any man who maintains such a belief, regardless of race, is stupid. The human female is a goddess who should be cherished, honored, and respected by *all* men. So, any man who preys on a woman for sex does not give a damn about that woman. His ill treatment of his woman is what *makes* him stupid.

Malik

Similar to Ralph and Kendall, Malik, a man in his 30s, also preys on women. But what makes Malik different is that he targets Black Women, both young and older, who are deemed "ugly" by American society. Malik claims to have been faithful in all of his past relationships with Black Women, but he got dumped by the woman of his dreams, who was drop-dead gorgeous. After this, he vowed to play the dating game until he meet the new lady of his dreams, whom he envisions as the complete opposite of his gorgeous ex in every way imaginable. He admitted to me that he seeks out ugly girls because they do not remind him of his ex. But this is not the only reason. I asked him to elaborate on other reasons why he targets unattractive women, and the first thing he said was this: "Ugly women are easy to manipulate, so it's *nothing* to get inside their heads, put them on an emotional rollercoaster, and take them back to my crib. When I see a group of Black Women hanging out, I automatically go for the ugliest one. After a few compliments, she's all in. I fuck her before the month's out, and then I'm gone—on to the next one." To prove his point, Malik showed me a stack of about 100 photos. And, to my surprise, every single photo in this stack was of a different woman. And *all* of them were what society would consider unattractive.

I then asked Malik if he believed what he was doing to these Black Women was ethical. "This has nothing to do with morality," he said. "It's all about getting my dick wet in the easiest way possible. We all have preferences, and this is mine." He has himself brainwashed to believe that mental and emotional manipulation of unattractive women is the key to sexual bliss. He does not even realize how stupid he is.

Leon

Leon is a 21-year-old college student who I met rather recently. Unlike Malik, he prefers to target highly attractive women, especially those who are light-skinned. To my question, "What drives your desire to target very beautiful women?" Leon responded as follows: "What drives my desire is a need to make bad bitches crack. They often think they're too much, and I like proving them wrong." He went on to say, "Gorgeous women are easy to deceive. Deny them attention, and they go out of their way to enter your world. I use reverse psychology and tell them they're not all that, and I *treat'em* that way. And, before I know it,

I be *diving* in their pussy." I asked him if he believed that Black Women should be treated better than that, and his response was, "After everything that Black broads put a nigga through, they should be *glad* that a nigga still talking to'em. Most of 'em don't *deserve* to be treated any better, especially the bourgeois ones. So I ain't got no love for'em. I lie to'em, fuck'em, then leave'em."

Men like Leon are seen everywhere, it seems, especially down here in the South. They both love *and* hate beautiful, light-skinned Black Women, and they find pleasure in manipulating and hurting them, taking advantage of their minds and emotions. This kind of stupid behavior aimed toward *any* Black Woman only creates tension among Black Women and Men. Men like Ralph, Kendall, Malik, and Leon do not care about Beautiful Black Love, and this is killing us as a people.

Problems Caused by Mind and Emotion Manipulation

A list of problems caused by mind and emotion manipulation could probably go on for pages but, generally, there are only about five major problems. It is these primary problems that I will elaborate on in this section. These five problems are:

1. Emotional turmoil and confusion that leads to defense mechanism creation, erratic behavior, and trust issues.
2. Misguidance that results in lashing out upon manipulation discovery, and placement of self as secondary in importance where there is no such discovery.
3. Mental debilitation and stagnation of mental and emotional development.
4. Discouragement that leads to doubt and low self-esteem.
5. Alteration of male perception.

Now, let us discuss these problems.

Emotional Turmoil and Confusion

Usually, before women are taken advantage of by manipulative men, they are the sweetest, kindest creatures on earth. Relationships of all kinds shared with them are fruitful. Their emotions are usually well-balanced. But, after they are deceived and used by men, their emotions go haywire. They become so confused while trying to figure out how they ended up in such a bad situation that they lose the purest parts of themselves. From this point on, as a means of avoiding any further emotional distress, they engage in protective mental activity. They construct countless mental barriers, create complex defense mechanisms. This makes it really hard for a man to get to know them on a personal level, which causes some good men to lose interest in them.

Many times, however, a woman may suspect that she is being mentally and emotionally manipulated by a man, and she may even flat out *know* this, but she refuses to leave that man because the manipulation feels good. So she sticks with him because she is addicted to feeling good. And, in the process, her behavior changes. She become unpredictable, doing things she would not normally do. But, when she realizes what is happening, if she dumps that man, her trust from that point on is never again given to a man freely. She flees from any man she even *suspects* will dishonor her trust.

Misguidance

Women who fall for the charms of manipulators lose their sense of self-guidance and usually rely on the manipulative men they are with to lead them. They hope and even believe that these men will guide them in the right directions but the opposite always seems to happen: they eventually end up in a fucked up situation, wondering how in the hell they got there. But, before they discover this, they are usually so far gone and deluded by deception that they, in many ways, put these men before themselves, and sometimes even before their own children. Women like this assume a secondary status while their men become the primary focus of importance. These women go out of their way to keep their men happy, even at the expense of their own misfortune, while the man basks in his newfound glory. But, when the ruse is up, these women are so hurt and distraught that they lash out verbally, emotionally, and even physically. But they do not just lash out at the men who deceived them, they do it to almost every man they meet after that, the good *and* the bad ones. Typically, these are the women who are overanalytical, super inquisitive, and straight up paranoid. I have been with a lot of women like this.

Mental Debilitation and Stagnation

The mind of a woman who is manipulated by a man, especially a man who just wants to get between her thighs, becomes weak. And this problem only worsens when a woman has gone from one manipulative man to another. Why? Because the mind itself needs room to grow. If it is constantly being manipulated, it never truly reaches its full potential. The same goes for emotions. Therefore, the mind and emotions of such a woman become stagnated. As a result, she usually finds herself in the same kind of a relationship, with the same kind of manipulative man, going through the same thing—all the time. Her mind and emotions are not evolving. So, if and when she *does* meet a good, non-manipulative man, she will run him away. This is because her mind and emotions are, for a lack of better words, subnormal and substandard in comparison to his. In addition to having drawn this conclusion from my own research on this subject, I know this from personal experience, because I have left *many* women after becoming aware of their mental and emotional stagnation. I would try my hardest to help them evolve, but to no avail. So I fled without thinking twice about looking back.

Discouragement

One of the most obvious indications that a woman has been mentally and emotionally manipulated by a man, especially if all that man wanted was sex, is her words and behavior that reveal overt signs of self-doubt, low self-esteem, reluctance to enter relationships, and avoidance of love—and/or marriage—related discussion. I have noticed this a lot with such women. These women are also very reluctant to have sex. They have a general loss of optimism. They question whether they are good enough for the men they meet because, if they are not good enough for them, they believe these men may also manipulate them. And the reason women like this have low self-esteem is that they believe that only women who are not worth a damn are manipulated in the way(s) that they were manipulated. So they are reluctant to have sex, enter relationships, and discuss love and relationships because they are afraid of being manipulated and taken advantage of again. They do not want to take any chances. Consequently, these women hinder themselves from finding true love.

Alteration of Male Perception

A man who deliberately seeks out women to manipulate mentally and emotionally just to have sex with them does more than just scorn them for life—he sometimes alters these women's entire perception of men. Before such women are manipulated, they see man as woman's companion. They know men are not perfect, but they still give them a chance at love. But, after being taken advantage of, they perceive men as inconsiderate assholes who would do and say anything to get a woman to have sex with them. Some of these women grow to hate men so much that they begin to test the waters of lesbianism. I have seen this with my own eyes.

All of the problems mentioned above occur when stupid men take advantage of women by way of mind and emotion manipulation. All five of these problems may not occur with all manipulated women, because each woman's situation is unique. But most women who have been manipulated by men can relate to experiencing at least one of these problems. But the subject of Stupid Black Men does not stop here, as you will soon see. So read on. Turn to the next chapter!

Chapter Four

Relationship Parasites

It seems as if, in our contemporary American society, only women come to mind when one hears the term "gold digger." First and foremost, I believe the cause of this is found in our own lexicon, where "gold digger" refers only to women. And many of our children grow up believing that only females are or can be gold diggers. I have in front of me the third edition of *The American Heritage High School Dictionary,* and in it the informal term "gold digger" is defined as follows: "A woman who seeks money and expensive gifts from men." This definition is passed down from generation to generation by way of our so-called "American heritage" and, even though times have changed, no one seems to even question this. The truth is that, in our day and age, as many women can and would surely attest, there exist countless men who seek money and expensive gifts from women, especially in the Black community—where women are usually more educated and financially stable than those of the opposite sex. Such men are more than just gigolos (who receive financial compensation and support in return for just sex) because, usually sex honestly does not dominate these men thoughts—money does. And it is this truth that makes them male gold diggers. Most of these men end up in relationships with women who have more money than them, and usually better jobs. Sometimes they only stay with these women until they accomplish whatever financial-related goal they came to accomplish, but oftentimes they tend to stick around for quite a while. They perpetuate the illusion of love, all the while sucking their women dry, which is why I call such gold digging men "relationship parasites."

If one really, I mean *really*, pays attention to a relationship, it is fairly easy to pinpoint a relationship parasite. He usually flatters his woman a lot and fucks her really good while habitually taking advantage of her generosity without making any useful return. Every now and then he makes some kind of contribution, but it is just a game, a play to convince his woman that he is really trying his best to take care of his share of half of the relationship's responsibility. Just pay attention, and you will see this. I see it now, and I have been seeing this all of my life. I have known a surprisingly large number of men who viewed women as their ticket out of some kind of bad situation, be it poverty, debt, or some other relevant predicament. All these men do is use women to get where they want to be financially. Of course, men do not tell women this. But they have no problem admitting it in a boastful manner to other men, especially if *those* men are also living off *their* women. Therefore, on my journey to acquire information from such men, I knew it would be best to seek out the most arrogant Black male gold diggers I could find. I was in luck, so to speak, because I encountered *a lot* of such arrogant men. As I do with all of my interviewees when I am conducting a survey, I informed these men that it is highly likely that whatever they said would be published in one of my books, but I would keep their identities anonymous. All of the men I surveyed/interviewed for this chapter found no problem at all with telling me whatever I wanted to know regarding the subject at hand. In fact, they were *eager* to tell it all. One guy even told me that he did not mind me using his real name and identity, because he "has his bitch so brainwashed that she would think the book was talking about two people from another state who just happen to have the same names as they do." I will keep the identities of his wife and him anonymous, but check out what he and a few other men like him had to say about being male gold diggers and relationship parasites.

Earl

Earl is a construction worker who is in his late 30s. After explaining to him my overall take on the male gold digger/relationship parasite subject, I asked Earl, "Which would you consider yourself most, a gold digger or a relationship parasite?" This is what he said: "Man, I'm *both*! But I'm more of a gold digger who found gold in my relationship. My wife is a breadwinner, a go-getter. And I put it down right, so she takes care of me. I'm a hustler, too, so I follow the money. And, right now, she just happens to be that money." I then asked him, "Aside from you being a 'hustler' and 'following the money,' what other reasons explain why you do what you do?" He answered as follows: "Man, look at the economy. It's hard out here, especially for Black men like myself. I got laid off from my last job and must've submitted a million applications to a bunch of employers. No one's hiring. But these broads out here, *they* are the ones getting hired, the ones with the money. So, if they want me, they got to pay. I'm trying to survive." Earl seemed to be completely open and honest, so I then asked him a rather blunt question. "Did you marry your wife for love or money and, if for money, do you love her?" I asked. His response was, "Man, I married her for the *money*. I mean, I wouldn't say I'm *in* love with her. I *do* feel a *little* something for her. But, at the end of the day, for me, it's all about the dollars."

Earl and I went on talking for quite some time, as I took notes. At the end of our little session, I asked him what did he have to say to other men out there in the world who do what he does to women, and if he felt like what he does makes him unmanly. This is what he said: "All I have to say to other men like me is this: keep your bitch brainwashed, and keep putting that dick down right. If you don't, your money's going to leave.

And, no, I don't feel like I'm less of a man, because a real man does whatever he has to in order to survive. And I'm surviving. Broads do the same thing I'm doing to dudes all the time. Why can't I do the same?"

I left my interview with Earl knowing in my heart that he will probably never change, which means that, somewhere down the line, some other Black Woman somewhere will also be taking care of all his financial needs, brainwashed by his deception. Then the next day, I talked to another male gold digger who we will call Desmond. He was worse than Earl.

Desmond

Desmond is the same age that I am at the time of this writing—29. He graduated from high school, went to college and acquired a Bachelor's degree in Business Administration, and has even had some admirable jobs. My overall opinion is that, judging from all that he told me, he does not have to live off *anybody* to be financially stable. He is very intelligent and charismatic, would do damn well on his own. I told him this, but his mind is made up. He has a particular goal in mind and sees male gold digging as the only way to accomplish it. Therefore, he is absolutely content with being a relationship parasite.

Desmond has been with his girlfriend (let us call her Vicky) for four years now. Vicky is several years older than he is, and her "finances are superb and about to put him exactly where he needs to be" successfully. They met each other on a blind date after one of Desmond's friends told him that "Vicky comes from money and has lots of connections." So he was after her money from day one. They hit it off. After Vicky told him about her last boyfriend, Desmond researched him and found out that he had

Vicky so far gone in love that, when he threatened to leave her, she almost went broke trying to convince him to stay. And this is when Desmond came up with a plan: Make her fall in love, then threaten to leave her, and use all her money to open his dream business—then leave her for real. He said that he is currently in "stage three," because she has given him full access to her bank accounts, and he is currently drawing up the building plans for his business. In a question and answer format, here is how part of our discussion went:

Me: "You are obviously intelligent, and you have awesome work experience, so why do you choose to live off a woman for financial stability?"

Desmond: "When I was growing up, I went to live with my dad every summer. My mom was busting her ass to pay the bills, but my dad didn't have a problem. He was with a different chic every summer, in a different house, and always had more money than he did the previous summer. And he always told me that, if I always had a chic with money, I would never want for anything."

Me: "Where is your dad now?"

Desmond: "In Florida, in a two-story house, with a chic who has *a lot* of money. They have five cars, and he runs all of their businesses. He wants for nothing."

Me: "Okay, so you believe your father's situation proves that living off of women is right?"

Desmond: "It's *more* than right—it necessary."

Me: "How so?"

Desmond: "Because men were put on this earth to rule, and a lot of these women out here who have money don't know what to do with it. We have to *think* for women, because they can't really think for themselves."

Me: "What would you do if your girl found out you were playing her for her money?"

Desmond: "She *won't* find out. You can't tell her I'm not an angel. It's too late now, anyway, because all the money's mine. Like you say, I'm a 'relationship parasite.' That's true. But, in a few months, when my business is up and running and I cut her out everything, *she's* going to be the parasite living off of men to get back everything I took from her. That's life, so she's going to have to charge it to the game, got to work her way back up."

As Desmond talked, his whole aura revealed that he is so devoted to his goal of being successful that he does not love or even care about his girlfriend. To him, she is nothing but a stepping stone he uses to get where he wants to be in life. I did not remember to ask him if he loves Vicky. His response would have probably been, "No," followed by a sly smirk.

Terrence

Terrence is a dude from the 'hood. He reminds me of a particular chic who once tried to trap my brother by claiming that she was pregnant and the unborn child was his. The only difference is that Terrence is male instead of female. I believe that the chic that did this to my brother had been scoping him out and plotting that since the day she met him. And, as soon as she thought she had him, she made her move. Well, Terrence is the same way. His wife, who I will call Shontel, was his ticket out of the streets and into the suburbs. She was his "meal ticket."

Shontel moved down to New Orleans, Louisiana, from California when she was 19. She was one of those people who believed that, because New Orleans is located in the "deep south," dudes from the Big Easy were very country and behind time, not as "on point and game tight" as guys in California. What she did not know is that, though that assumption might have applied to many other Louisianans, New Orleans was and is an entirely different and unique kind of city, filled to capacity with shrewd men whose tongues could "spit game a million different ways." Shontel sought to "catch" Terrence and take him back with her to California. She has since been "captured" by him, and they now live in the suburbs out of state.

Anyway, in brief, after wooing Shontel, Terrence "came up." Nearly every penny of the large amounts of money Shontel regularly received from her parents back home was either spent on or given to Terrence. So he stopped selling drugs and committing armed robberies, then fled New Orleans with her for good. He told me that he scoped her out from day one, saw that she was "green," as in gullible and ripe for the picking, then he moved in for the kill. He considers what he has done to Shontel "a Big Easy checkmate." Following are a few quotes from all of the things he told me:

> "You're from New Orleans, so you already know how it is down there. Them slums ain't what's happening. And I *love* money. So, if I meet a ho with money, I gotta get her."
> "I was off in the streets, robbing niggas, slanging that dope, and getting blood money. How long you think I was gon' last? If I wouldn't have ran game on Shontel and made her my wife, I'd probably be dead or in jail right now." "My ho *take care* of me, son. And, if she ever stop kicking out that cash, I'mma leave that ho—quick. I love her, but that's how it is. If it don't make money, it don't make sense."

In my younger days, I was so deep into the streets and the "hood" thing that, had I met Terrence then, I would have been giving him dap after dap, congratulating him on a job well done regarding Shontel. But, after leaving that life, everything Terrence said sounds stupid to me. In truth, it does not make sense if everything is just about making money, because God and love are the most powerful things in the universe. It shames me that so many of my Black brothers are so materialistic that they are willing to treat like rag dolls the very creatures that birthed them into existence. That is utter insanity, but it is what we are dealing with in Black America.

Men like Earl, Desmond, and Terrence think that living off women is cool. And there are *so* many men doing this these days that this wicked, unnatural way of life is spreading like wildfire amongst Black Men here in the states, especially since so many Black Women are increasingly becoming more well-educated in a great variety of fields, which puts a lot more money in their pockets. So this is a serious problem that just causes more and more problems for our Beautiful Black Women.

Problems Caused by Relationship Parasites

Of all of the problems relationship parasites cause, the following problems are the worst:

1. Major setbacks that damage and sometimes utterly destroy future success.
2. Creation of overexaggerated, financially independent views and attitudes.
3. Perpetuation of the Black-Man-as-underachiever stereotype.

Now, let us elaborate on these problems.

Major Setbacks

In our society, and especially in Black communities, Black Women learn very early in life that a promising future only comes by way of diligent planning and self-sacrifice, unless one is just born into a privileged family, which is not usually the case for Black Women. So they grow up working hard as hell to make sure that they are able to live life comfortably when they grow old. By the time they enter their adult years, they have their entire lives planned out to a T. So, nearly everything they do after that is advancing them toward their goals—and then some stupid ass Black Man comes along. He deceives them into investing their future and finances in him, then one day they wake up and realize that everything they worked so hard for is gone, Now they have to start all over, rebuild what he destroyed. They are back to square one. Some women, particularly those who are young, are able to start over and reacquire what they lost, but many older women cannot because their productive years are almost over. Consequently, they never truly shake back from this experience.

Over-Exaggeration of Financial Independence

After a woman has been robbed blind by a man, she oftentimes develops a strong sense of financial independence, always sure to guard her wealth from men so that she will never be misused in such a way again. This is a good thing. But the downside to this is that, over time, scorned women have a tendency to let their financial independence go to their heads, causing them to go over and beyond to prove that they are financially independent and do not need a man to do anything for them money-wise. They act stuck up and start rubbing their independence in men's faces, which only alienates men. So, whenever a good man *does* come along, their boasting of independence only compels him to flee them. Now they are manless, lonely, and void of that beautiful thing called love—all because a previous man that they loved and trusted turned out to be a relationship parasite. It is hard for them to let go of this and move on.

The Black Man as Underachiever

Because of all of the other stupid shit that Black Men do, Black Women usually go through life struggling to trust Black Men who are alleged to be and do all kinds of bad things. They hear a lot of negative things about the opposite sex: Black Men are unfaithful by nature, they cannot be trusted, and all they do is think with their dicks. Of course, these things are not true for every Black Man. But, when large numbers of Black Men are constantly robbing their Beautiful Black Women blind, what is a Black Woman to believe? She has no other choice but to believe that Black Men are lazy underachievers who are incapable of doing what women do. And this only makes Black Men look stupid in the eyes of the public. And, if *they* look stupid, how do you think people view their women? They view them as stupid as well.

As you can see, relationship parasites cause all kinds of problems for their women. The only way to stop this is to stop such men from doing stupid, gold digging-related things. But, as you will see as you read on, Black Male Stupidity does not stop here. It gets a lot worse. You will witness this in the next chapter.

Chapter Five

Jealous Black Men
in Relationships

"I understand that this is a free country and all, that women share and are entitled to the same rights that we have as men, but I'll be *damned* if I let some woman I'm with make more money than me. So, if my woman starts bringing in most of the income in our household, if I can't get a raise or find a job with better pay, then she will have to either quit her job or demote herself to a lower position at work. If she refuses, I'm leaving."

The above quote comes from a survey I conducted in the latter part of 2011. In the survey, I had some questionnaires mailed out to random Black Men regarding Black Men who become jealous when their women start bringing home the bacon. The guy who stated this in writing has been married for over twenty years and proudly maintains that he is "very old school when it comes to moneymaking in relationships." He also says that, as a young boy, he was taught that husbands are supposed to be providers, and women should stay home and take care of their families. Today, many old heads like him still exist.

This country has changed in *so* many ways during the past three decades. There is a large generational gap between the old and the young. It may seem to some people that, because of this generational gap, old heads such as the one mentioned above have not really been able to pass their beliefs down to the younger generation. But, somehow and some way, these beliefs have definitely been adopted by men my age and younger. These younger men, however, do not maintain these beliefs as adamantly as their older counterparts. Nevertheless, the very existence of such inherited beliefs causes women to be mistreated and looked down upon as inferior.

I will not quote any rap songs, but if you listen to a lot of the stuff that many rappers are saying, it becomes evident that they believe women should not be breadwinners in any kind of a relationship. And, because rap is one of the most—if not *the* most—popular genres of music in this country, this belief is being adopted by Black Men across the nation. What I have noticed, though, is that most men who maintain this belief, both young and old, are usually not too eager to reveal it. Therefore, most women do not discover it until their men get jealous and start "acting funny" when wealth acquisition is mastered by the woman in the relationship.

Jealous-Based Actions and Behaviors

Men in America have a tendency to act overly macho instead of just being themselves, and this is taken to an extreme amongst Black Men, many of whom have mastered acting tough. This is true for Black Men in the suburbs and in middle-class neighborhoods as it is for Black Men in the ghetto. The only difference is that these men act tough in different ways. More than in any other way, I have seen this a lot during my time in prison. Guys who are considered gangsters, thugs, and heartless killers come behind these fences, walls, and bars and turn wimp after a certain amount of mental and physical pressure is applied to them. They just crack. Consequently, the ones who once told other men to "stop acting like a bitch" thus become the bitches—sometimes literally. And, in many ways, this is the same thing that happens to a lot of Black Men in relationships with breadwinning Black Women. Their actions and behaviors change. They go from kind, sweet, and strong to envious, jealous, and bitter. They just transform all of a sudden.

After the survey I did on this subject with men, I decided to do another survey on the same subject, but this time with all Black Women. So I put the word out that I was conducting research on this matter and would love to hear some accounts from women that validate my assertions. Shortly after, many of my Beautiful Black Sisters came running! They *flooded* me with information on this subject and told of their encounters with jealous Black Men with whom either they or their closest friends and relatives had once been involved. So here are some of their stories.

Iyana

Iyana is 32 years old and has been a breadwinner all her life. She said her dad, though he was the breadwinner in their household, always encouraged her to be a go-getter when she was a little girl. He told her that women can do anything men can do, and are oftentimes better than men. So she grew up with an air of confidence about her, knowing that she would be like her dad—a breadwinner. She has two business degrees and is recently divorced. I asked her to tell me what caused her divorce. She said her ex-husband "cheated for recreation." However, she also said that the real problems between them started when she was promoted to a new position at work. Prior to her promotion, they were bringing in about the same amount of income. But the promotion she received officially made her the chief moneymaker of the relationship. Here is an excerpt from an interview I conducted with her.

Me: "What kind of changes did you see in him (her husband, who we will call Tyrone) after you got your promotion?"

Iyana: "Well, at first, he tried to act like everything was all cool, like he was happy for me. He even went so far as to take me out to a restaurant and throw me a party. But about a month or two after that, the truth started coming out."

Me: "What happened?"

Iyana: "We would get certain bills in the mail, bills that we usually either pay together or divide and pay separately. But all of a sudden now, he wants *me* to pay the costliest bills myself because now I'm making more money."

Me: "Were there any other signs?"

Iyana: "Yes, a *bunch* of signs. He started teasing me in front of everybody, both my family and my friends, calling me his 'little Ms. Piggybank.' They all thought what he was doing was cute, but I know the *real* meaning behind it—he was jealous. He also started spending money on stupid things just so he wouldn't have enough money to pay his share of the bills, so I could cover it all. He was also acting childish. He was playing all kinds of games."

Me: "What was the worst part of it all?"

Iyana: "When we started arguing about all this, and the arguments got really serious. I couldn't take it anymore, and told him I won't pay his share of the bills, that he needed to man up. He would always get mad and storm off like a little girl. I was more of a man than him. Anyway, the arguments tore us apart, and that's when he started cheating, I got *more* than my half of everything after the divorce, so I'm good (smiles). The last thing he told me was that none of this would've happened if I would've refused my promotion. He tried to blame it on me, like it is *my* fault."

See what I mean about Black Men being stupid? Guys like Tyrone end up losing out on Beautiful Black Love because they cannot control their emotions. He should have supported and encouraged his woman after she got promoted. She *earned* that. Instead, he decided to act like a sissy—just stupid. Another woman I talked to, Ashley, once went through something similar with an ex boyfriend, who we will call Calvin. I must mention that Ashley, like me, grew up in poverty but made it out of the 'hood by way of smart decisions. She loves to use the N-word, though. I tend to keep it one hundred percent real in my books, so I have decided not to omit the N-word from the following excerpt. Here is Ashley's story.

Me: "How did you become the breadwinner in your relationship with Calvin?"

Ashley: "I was on the cheerleading squad in high school when I met Calvin. He was out there hustling, selling drugs, making a lot of money. He told me he'd give me anything I wanted, so I told him to pay my way into college, and that nigga *did* it. He took care of me. Then he went to jail, and I used the money he left to open a business when I turned 21. I took care of him the whole time he was in, so I was the breadwinner when he got out—and that's when that nigga started tripping."

Me: "In what ways did he trip?"

Ashley: "When he got out, the whole parole thing was frustrating for him. He couldn't find a job. The only work experience he had was hustling, so he relied on me for financial support. And that drove that nigga crazy, especially after I got pregnant and had Asia, our daughter, because most of the stuff he bought her, he got the money from me. And he was too afraid of going back to jail, so he didn't hustle. So he started making all kinds of fake ass comments, like, 'I shouldn't have left you all my money,' and stuff like that. Then his behavior changed completely, and the nigga was getting on my last nerve, trying to make me feel guilty. Since his drug money got me where I am, I *was* going to give him half of everything, the business *and* the money. But, when he started acting like that, I was, like, 'Fuck that nigga.' Then we just grew apart or whatever. This went on for years until we split."

Me: "How did his behavior change, I mean, besides the comments?"

Ashley: "I mean, obviously, he was straight up jealous. So he started trying to find lots of ways to make more money than me. But that didn't work out, because of his criminal record. He didn't want to touch me anymore. So he stopped kissing me, and we stopped having sex. I suspected he was cheating, but the nigga was so slick, so I never got any real proof. And he tried to turn Asia against me, my own daughter. It was just crazy. Now he's back in jail—alone."

Me: "What would you tell Calvin right now if he were in front of you?"

Ashley: "That he's stupid! I was down for him, he *had me,* but he let his ego get in the way of what we had, all because I was making all the money, and not him, like he was so used to doing. But that's just life. A nigga is going to be a nigga regardless. I guess that's just how it goes."

I agree with Ashley about Calvin being stupid, because only a stupid man would do what he did. I mean, not only did that

Beautiful Black Woman hold him down, but she was going to keep it real and give him half of everything. So for him to behave in the manner in which he behaved, he had to have been stupid. He threw away Beautiful Black Love, knew not the wonders of BBL, which is why he is in the predicament that he is in now. Anyway, moving on, meet Mrs. Darlene, an older Black Woman with her own story to tell.

Mrs. Darlene

Darlene is a very sweet-natured, amazing Black Woman. Though over sixty years old, she looks not a day over 40. And she is quite gorgeous. I will never forget her because her very dark, ebony skin is the most beautiful skin I have ever seen, and her demeanor exudes elegance. She reminds me of King Tut's dark-skinned grandmother, Queen Tiy, because Tiy was a strong Black Woman. Darlene is more beauteous in appearance, though.

Anyway, Darlene is happily married to her second husband, Cedric. Their 20-plus years of marriage have been fruitful from day one. But her first husband, William, put her through hell. She said they had always had problems, but "the foolishness just got out of hand" after William suffered a certain work-related injury that prevented him from working for several years. Here is an excerpt from an interview I conducted with her.

Me: "Tell me about William before and after the work-related injury?"
Darlene: "Well, like I told you earlier, William and I had always had problems. But, despite that, before the injury, we still had lots of good times together. We would go out all the time, have in-home Bible studies. And I was

young back then, so we ummm . . . 'rolled in the hay' a lot (she laughs, meaning they had sex). I was a secretary at this time, and he was a manager at a large construction company, getting paid top dollar, *way* more money than I was. But then the accident happened; he couldn't work. I had to take care of him in a lot of ways, including financially. He was traditional in thinking and *hated* having to depend on a woman for money, so he became really hateful towards me."

Me: "In what ways did his hate manifest?"

Darlene: (Her countenance now saddened) "He started physically abusing me, saying that he would 'beat all of that pride out of me.' He thought I was proud to be the one making all the money, which wasn't true one bit. I told my family about what he was doing, some of my uncles paid him a visit, and I haven't seen or heard from him since. But one of my old girlfriends told me that she saw him at a big church in Texas, with his new wife. Rumor has it that he is hitting her, too."

By physically abusing Darlene, William took his jealousy to the extreme. He is stupid for how he treated her. He treated her like trash, but she is now another man's treasure. Unfortunately, not all women like Darlene get another chance at finding BBL, because their first encounter with men like William destroys them for life. Sometimes the same is true for women who end up in relationships with men like Tyrone and Calvin. I can go on and on with more stories that provide more and more examples of such men, but I think you get the picture. Many of these so-called grown men in our Black communities, especially these youngsters who run around proclaiming to be men, are so selfish, prideful, egotistical and weak that they hate to see their Beautiful Black Women moving up in the world financially. And, when they start acting all funny and end up losing their women for good, this causes problems for both them *and* their women. The women's problems become worse.

Problems Caused by Jealous Men

Men who get jealous and change their behavior in an unmanly manner after their women become breadwinners cause the following problems:

1. They make women question their status as women.
2. They create in women a diminishment of male perception.
3. They cause women to seek out men of equal or similar wealth while neglecting good, strong men who are less financially stable than they are.

Of course, these three problems are not the only problems caused by such men, but they are the major ones.

Women's Questioning of Self-Status

Women are born into this world superior to men in a lot of ways, but men do everything in their power to brainwash them into believing that men are superior to women. And, because men control most of earth's wealth and natural resources, and almost everything else on the earth, an illusion of male superiority permeates the globe. Women, therefore, have to work twice as hard as men to be successful. So, when they fall in love with men whom they believe perceive them as equals, then those seemingly strong-minded men start downplaying their women's success, many women question whether they are in fact meant to play second fiddle to men. Some women get past this, but others do not. Those of the latter category thus fall into the trap of thinking that everything will return to normal if they let their men take the lead. A persistent sense of inadequacy overtakes them, and they diminish themselves in a variety of ways. I have witnessed this a number of times. Women like this have an inferiority complex when it comes to gender—related issues, and this kills the equality between man and woman.

Diminishment of Male Perception

Prior to becoming jealous and behaving in an unmanly manner after his woman starts making more money than he does, a man is usually perceived by his woman positively. She may view him as a strong, mature, very manly kind of man. But, when he starts acting all "boyish," hating on his woman because of her financial success, her perception of him as a man changes, because she knows that real men do not behave this way. He thus becomes immature in her eyes. This is understandable. Therefore, when such a woman learns of other men who have behaved the same, her relationships with other men are affected by her change in male perception. Those men may be the epitome of real men, but she will almost always be on guard, wondering if they will start behaving in the same way the men she had before them behaved.

The Seeking of Men with Equal or Similar Wealth

Most women, especially Black Women, do not want to experience the same kind of pain and disappointment twice. So, when their relationships with jealous men that hated having them as breadwinners end, they sometimes refuse to date men who are less financially stable than they are. Rather, they neglect such men by dating only those who have either the same amount, or a similar amount, of money as they have. Because of this, they limit their options, which means that real love seems to take forever to find them. And, without real love, despite how much money they have, they never truly feel complete. But it is not their fault. The stupid, jealous Black Man is to blame.

Black Men who become jealous and allow their jealously to make them hateful toward their women are not real men. Real men *love* to see their women succeed, be it financially or otherwise. Therefore, any Black Man who argues the contrary argues only on the basis of flat out stupidity.

Chapter Six

Desertion of the
Black Mother and Child

I grew up in a single-parent home, so I know exactly what it is like to have a parent absent from a home. For as long as I can remember, my *mother* was my father. At least she tried her best to be, for which I honor and respect her a lot. However, when it came down to being a man, that was something my mother could never really teach me, so I had to find manhood on my own. I was lost for many years as a boy, just trying to find my way. As a result, I did not find manhood until the age of 25. Prior to this, I would oftentimes look at other young Black Men who grew up in fatherless homes and wonder why we all were so much alike—rebellious, selfish, immature, seemingly existing with no known life purpose to fulfill. Then I would look at older guys who were the opposite of what we were—goal-oriented, disciplined, mature, and cognizant of their mission in life—and wonder what made them so different. I later found out that most of these guys, either all their lives or at least at some point in their lives, grew up with fathers or father figures in their households. And not just fathers or father figures, but positive Black male role models. This is when I realized that, for boys, having a father or father figure is essential for proper life development and maturation. Usually, where there is no father, there is thus no guided path to manhood. And a man ignorant of manhood oftentimes propagates stupidity.

In my research, I have found that a significant number of Stupid Black Men either grew up in fatherless homes or had a father in their homes who were not truly fathers at all, meaning that they did not handle their paternal responsibilities well. I have also found that most Black Men who abandon their children and their children's mothers were similarly abandoned as well. I call this the "cycle of fatherlessness." And the Black Men who are perpetuating this cycle are all around us. They are found among the rich, the middle class, and the poor. Deserters of Black mothers and children are *everywhere*. Knowing this, during my research for this chapter, I sought out Black Men who have abandoned their children. I hoped they would be willing to be real with themselves and explain, on the record, why they decided to abandon their children and their children's mothers. However, only a few of these men were man enough to own up to what they have done. To my great disappointment, the majority of these men came up with a million different excuses in their attempts to justify their unmanly actions. Many times, during my interviews with these so-called men, I wanted to just stop the interviews and tell them to get the hell out of my face. But, for the sake of my Beautiful Black Women, I decided to stay focused so that I can put this stupidity on display, hoping that, by doing so, Black Men's awareness of Black Male Stupidity itself would ultimately abolish or de-escalate the magnitude of Black Male Stupidity in Black America. Only time will tell what will happen regarding the de-escalation of such stupidity. In the meantime, let me show you just how stupid some Black deadbeat dads are.

Shawn

Meet Shawn, a twentysomething guy from an urban community in Florida. He has four children, all of whom were born of different women. Prior to each child's birth, Shawn was involved in an intimate relationship with each child's mother. But, after each pregnancy, he abandoned each woman and child. Now he is on child support, complaining about how much money he has to pay monthly for each child. In fact, he seems to care more about the money than the children he fathered. Here is an excerpt from my interview with him.

Me: "How many children do you have?"

Shawn: "Four. Three boys, and one girl."

Me: "What's your relationship with them like?"

Shawn: "I don't really have a real relationship with them. We talk from time to time, but it's nothing really serious. I take them out sometimes."

Me: "Why *don't* you have real relationships with them? And how often do you see them?"

Shawn: "All of my kids have different mothers, and their mothers and I don't really see eye to eye. I ain't with none of them no more. They try to keep the kids away from me as much as possible. It's cool, though. I ain't messed up about it."

Me: "I think any *real* father *should* be messed up about it. And why aren't you with any of them anymore? What happened between you and each of them?"

Shawn: "I let *all* of them know that I wasn't ready for no children, but they all did what they wanted to do. They all wanted to get pregnant, especially Ariel, my daughter's momma. She stopped taking birth control pills, talking about 'she forgot,' she forgot to take the pills. But I know she did that on purpose, so the pregnancy was *her* fault—not mine. That's why I left her. Donovan, my youngest boy, his momma, Tarriana, was kind of the same way. She hated fucking with condoms, but I always insisted. Then, one time, she was riding me, and I felt the rubber bust when I was about to bust a nut. I tried to pull out, but she locked me down and rode me until I came. She played games, so Donovan was her fault. So I left her, too. My third baby momma, Alexis, I think she gave me a rubber that had a hole in it, because I *never* cut [had sex with] her without a rubber. She denied it, but I ain't stupid. So I cut her off when she told me she was pregnant. And Janelle, my last baby momma, I don't know *how* she got pregnant, 'cause I just fucked her one time, with a rubber, while she was on birth control. I thought the baby wasn't mine, but the blood test said it is. But I left her because that shit happened too strange. Ain't no way she was supposed to get pregnant."

Me: "It seems as if you are shifting the blame to all of these women, as if you had nothing to do with any of this."

Shawn: "I didn't."

Me: "Okay, let's assume that all of this happened just like you said it happened, that they trapped you or whatever. If they indeed did what you say they did, then I can understand you not being involved with them intimately anymore. But does this justify you not making any true efforts to be a major part of your kids' lives?"

Shawn: "Yeah, it justifies it, because I don't want to be a part of nothing that I was trapped into having. In my own way, I love my kids, but the fact is that I didn't want them before they were born. And ain't no woman or no judge gonna force me to want something I never wanted to have anyway. I hate having to pay child support, all that money every month for each child. I could be doing other shit with my money, but I'd rather pay it than accept how they played me."

See how stupid Shawn is? A real man, even if he were trapped into fathering children, would not shift the bulk of the blame to the women who gave birth to his children. He would acknowledge and admit that he had sex with these women on his own volition. He would, most importantly, despite all that happened, make a serious effort to be a major part of his children's lives. This is what real men do. Thus, when men fail to do this, when they run away from their responsibility and make up excuses to explain why they ran away, they are the opposite of real, just plain old, fake, deadbeat dads. Shawn is a good example of this. There seems to be a million "Shawns" out there in urban communities. But, as aforementioned, such are found in middle-class and suburban communities as well.

Roland

Meet Roland, a Black man of 30-plus years who has one child, a teenage son. Roland is a college graduate who now lives in the same middle-class neighborhood he lived in growing up. He has a nice job, a nice house, drives a nice car, and dates lots of nice women. He is perfectly capable of raising a child. Yet, he absolutely refuses to develop a relationship with Roland Jr., his son. Here is an excerpt.

Me: "Earlier, you mentioned that your son's mother and you were once madly in love, that she was your first love. Well, why did you abandon her when she got pregnant, you know, if you loved her so much?"

Roland: "In a lot of ways, I don't even know why I did what I did. All I know is that, one day we were in love, and I was loving her hard. Then, the next day, I just had to go. When she told me she was pregnant, I was entering college, my tuition paid and everything. We agreed to wait until after college to have children, so when she dropped that bomb on me and told me she was pregnant, I guess I felt like she lied to me, like she betrayed our agreement. I told her to get an abortion so we can wait until after college, that a baby and a family would only mess our lives and our futures up. But she let her family and friends get in her head, and she kept the baby. I couldn't let her or a child mess my future up, so I broke up with her. She betrayed our promise. And I'm glad I left, too, because I'm living good right now. I wouldn't be living this good if I would've stayed with her. Besides, my son don't even know me. She got him calling another dude 'Daddy,' so it's too late anyway."

Me: "I understand what you're saying about your future and wanting to wait until after college. But, if you were so serious about your future, why didn't you practice celibacy until after college? And did you all even use protection during sex?"

Roland: "Sometimes we used protection, and sometimes we didn't. She wanted to use condoms *all* the time, and I didn't because I need to *feel* something. As far as celibacy, that's for monks and old catholic men who can't get hard anymore (laughs), and for nuns. Me, I was young and, like I said, I needed to *feel* something."

Me: "You don't feel like a lot of this is your fault because you convinced her to give up condoms sometimes, knowing that she wanted to use protection *all* the time? Have you ever thought that maybe you betrayed yourself by putting your girl in a position to get pregnant, just because you wanted to 'feel something'?"

Roland: "No, it wasn't, because, if *she* was so serious, she wouldn't have *allowed* me to have sex with her without a condom. So I don't think I betrayed myself. All she had to do was get an abortion."

Me: "Will you ever try to develop some kind of relationship with your son?"

Roland: "Nah, because I don't really have a reason to. He already has a father. If I ever get another woman pregnant, it'll be on *my* terms."

What makes Roland stupid is not only his refusal to accept his responsibility as a father, but also his self-seeking attitude. I understand his point about not wanting to disrupt his future or whatever but, once a baby is born, the present takes precedence over the future as mother and father decide what needs to be done concerning the newborn child. The child's birth changes everything. So Roland's constant focus on the future instead of his son is what made him stupid. He is "living good" right now, but he will most likely become filled with regret at some point later in life as Beautiful Black Love eludes him.

Donald

Donald is a very educated Brother who, though he was not reared in the suburbs, now lives in a suburban neighborhood. He is married to his wife, Shonda, with whom he has three children. But he also has another daughter that he fathered two years before meeting Shonda. He left Shelley, his daughter's mom, for Shonda after an argument they had. He has not turned back since, so his daughter, now seven years old, is growing up without a dad. He does not even want to spend time with her—at all. He just provides for her financially, forced to do so because he's on child support. Here is some of what he had to say during my interview with him.

Me: "Why exactly did you leave Shelley for Shonda? I don't think a simple argument caused that."

Donald: "She just started getting out of hand, had so many issues that had nothing to do with me. But, when we first met, she wasn't like that. It's like she just changed overnight when she found out she was pregnant. I never cheated on her or gave her any impression that I was cheating. Not to *my* knowledge, anyway. But I would come home from work and she'd be sniffing all over me, interrogating me, searching my pockets and my phone. One time she even followed me to work. She started accusing me of stuff. I was innocent, though. Then, when Donella [his daughter] was born, she thought I was out getting other people pregnant. This was after the argument me and Shelley had, and I left Shelly for her."

Me: "Damn, it seems as if you didn't even consider how all of this would affect your daughter."

Donald: "Nah, I considered it. But I *know* that she'll use even her own child against me if she had to, and I was right. Because of her, Donella *hates* me now. But I already saw this coming, so I left and knew it wouldn't make sense turning back. I have my *own* family now, so I'm over that. I'm sorry Donella had to get caught up in all that, but shit happens."

Me: "Damn, that's harsh. Do you even *love* Donella?"

Donald: "I love her as a child, but I don't know her anymore, so I don't feel the same way I used to feel about her. You might think that's harsh, but that's the truth."

Me: "What about Shelley, did you ever love her?"

Donald: "Yeah, in the beginning. But when she started going crazy, I really stopped knowing what love was, what it felt like, until I met Shonda."

Me: "Do you ever feel like you abandoned Shelley and your daughter?"

Donald: "No. I just left a bad situation. Shelly abandoned *herself*. They'll be all right."

Donald is so unforgiving that nothing, it seems, can change his mind and convince him to become active in his daughter's life. A real man would have sat down with Shelley and talked to her in order to try to find out exactly why she was behaving the way she was. A real man would *never* leave his daughter like that—only a stupid man would. Shawn, Roland, and Donald are only a few of a very significant number of Stupid Black Men who, for various groundless reasons, just up and abandon their Beautiful Black Women and children. And, when a Black Woman and child are abandoned, this, like all the other stupid things Stupid Black Men do, causes serious problems. In this case, the problems not only regard Black Women but also their children.

Problems Caused by Black Family Abandonment

When a Black Man abandons his child and his child's mother, primarily, this causes the following problems:

1. The abandoned mother is thrown into a parental quagmire, one in which she attempts to play two parental roles but can only play one.
2. The abandoned child experiences a stunt on maturational growth that results in an identity crisis.
3. Both the abandoned mother and child becomes highly susceptible to influence that leads to rash decisions made in desperation.

The Parental Quagmire

Procreation is by nature a thing of duality. It takes two people to generate offspring, and the offspring created is a recipient of dualistic inheritance, because it inherits fifty percent of its mother's traits, and fifty percent of its fathers. Offspring is thus burn into a world in which dual parenting is required for proper offspring development. So, when a man abandons his woman and child, his woman steps in to play his role. But she cannot do this, because by nature she is only able to play hers. She cannot be a father, but she tries her best to be one—to no avail. This creates dysfunction in the world of parenting. And, when parenting is dysfunctional, so is the child, particularly psychologically.

Stunt on Maturational Growth and Identity Crisis

Full maturation requires a dual parenting base. Without this, a child, particularly a boy, will go about life in absence of a key element of himself—an innate desire for maturity. This can only be passed down to a child by a father. Without it, a child cannot mature properly. Therefore, until either a father figure or life itself helps a child mature, the child's mind does not develop fast enough. He or she grows up without any real knowledge of self, does not know his or her role in society, and is confused regarding his or her priorities. This is an identity crisis. And children who lack knowledge of their own identities oftentimes go astray.

The Making of Rash Decisions

A lot of mothers who are abandoned by their child's father, after realizing that they cannot successfully play both parental roles, usually become desperate to find a father figure for their child. And, in this desperation, they sometimes make some unwise decisions regarding men, bringing not-so-good men into their lives and the life that child. And, a lot of abandoned children, when they grow up, to fill the void left by their fathers, usually make similar mistakes, bringing into their lives people who only make their situations worse. They mess their own lives up.

Surely, I can go on for many more pages explicating the problems caused by men who abandon their children and their children's mothers, but you get the picture. If the Stupid Black Men in our communities do not start owning up to their parental responsibilities, a real future for our Beautiful Black Children will not exist, and the majority of our Beautiful Black Women will have hearts void of Beautiful Black Love.

Chapter Seven

Distorted Perceptions
of Beauty

"To each his own. You like what you like, and I like what I like. I'm not into the 'natural beauty' thing. If a chic's hair isn't straight, we can't talk, because I'm not into the nappy head thing. And, if her ass it too big, dude, that's a complete turn off for me. The same goes for her nose and lips. I like petite, light-skinned women. Anything other than that is ugly—especially if she's dark-skinned."

About three weeks ago, I was interviewing one particular guy to get his perception of beauty on record. A friend of mine had told me that the guy, who is jet black in skin complexion, though he is Black, has an utter distaste for most Black Women. So I sent a note to the guy explaining what my new book is about and told him that I would like to interview him for this particular chapter. We met up the following day and, during the interview, the above quote is some of what he told me. As I sat in front of this guy listening to him talk, all I could think about was Willie Lynch and the brainwashing methods that he used to break the will and distort the perceptions of male and female slaves. According to the letter popularly known as "The Willie Lynch Address," on slave plantations, Lynch, among other things, would give favorable plantation jobs to light-skinned slaves, thereby causing all of the slaves to associate light skin with status and beauty. Lynch also, if I remember correctly, brainwashed the slaves into believing that straight hair is more beautiful than that which is kinky. Well, after slavery was abolished, these former slaves maintained most of their beliefs, which have since been passed down from generation to generation in our Black communities across the nation. This miseducation has spawned the inventions of everything from hair straightening products to skin bleaching creams, as well as worsened Black Men's perceptions of beauty. Thus, though we are living in 21st century America, the minds of significant numbers of Black Men are still stuck on the plantation. All of this crossed my mind during my interview with the above-mentioned Black Man. And, since then, I have found much more proof of this kind of Black Male Stupidity.

Shortly after this interview, by way of questionnaires, I surveyed a sizable number of Black Men regarding Black Women's so-called "status," based solely on what many Americans would consider to be beauty. What I discovered was that the overall majority of these Black Men believe that Black Women are inferior to not only white women but *all* women if their physical features do not meet the standards of traditional European-American beauty (that is, straight hair, small nose, small lips, thin physique, small butt, etc.). In this chapter, I will highlight a few men who possess what I believe to be the most commonly held perceptions maintained by a large number of Black Men here in America, although most of these men are afraid to admit this to Black Women. For each Black Man mentioned, I will highlight some of his written responses to particular survey questions.

Craig

Q: "In your opinion, what makes a Black Woman beautiful, that is, physically attractive?"

A: "It depends, because all women are different, and you know Black Women come in all sizes, shapes, and colors but, generally, my preference is long hair with a slim build. Not super anorexic slim, but sexy slim, petite. But sometimes I like them skinny too. And her hair has to be at least down to her shoulders. I like it down her back, though, as long as it's straight. I don't do women with dreadlocks, because dreadlocks are nasty. And, if her hair is naturally short, then she can use weave to lengthen it and make it *look* long. As long as her hair is long and straight, even if it's not real, and her body is slim, I'm good. Most Black Women like that are attractive to me, especially if they have style."

Q: "Do you prefer Black Women with large butts?"

A: "No. the big booty thing is overrated. I like a woman with a small booty that I can squeeze with my palms and it doesn't feel like a big basketball or something. That big booty thing is also unhealthy, because I know Black girls out here who eat a lot to keep a big booty. I don't like that."

Q: "Do you consider Black Women's noses and lips to be sexy characteristics?"

A: "It depends. If their noses and lips are big, no. If they are small, yes. Big noses and lips might be the thing in Africa, but not over here in America. I'm Black, but I like Black Women who are pretty in the *American* way. If she's good with the felatio, though, I might consider her. But, once she's done, she can kick rocks."

Kirk

Q: "Are you attracted to Black Women who prefer to wear their hair in natural, that is, cultural and unrelaxed styles?"

A: "This is 2012. All that 'Black Power, I'm-going-natural stuff' is dead. It's played out. If I approach a dame and her hair is anything other than straight and well-kept, I'm turning around. This happens to me a lot at nightclubs, because it's usually dark, I can't really see their hair in detail from across the room. It doesn't hurt to get a perm. That nappy shit is *not* what's up. Straight hair *is* the natural thing now. That's one of the reasons I be chasing these white girls. I can run my fingers through their hair without them getting stuck, and I can pull their hair during sex and know I'm pulling something real. I can't do that with too many Black broads because, if I pull their hair, the whole damned wig or weave might come off!"

Q: "Are light-skinned Black Women more beautiful than dark-skinned Black Women?"

A: "That's a no brainer because EVERYBODY knows that red bones are hotter than dark-skinned broads. That's why all I date is light-skinned chics. A lot of dark chics are ugly. And the blacker they are the uglier they are. I only know a couple pretty dark broads, but most light-skinned chics I know and see, if they ain't pretty, they ain't ugly either. Most of them look good. Why you think Jay Z got Beyoncé, T.I. got Tiny, and Lil Wayne had Toya? Them niggas sitting on top of the world with access to all kinds of dames, but they choose red bones. That's proof right there. At least that's how I see it."

Q: "Do you prefer Black Women to be 'fine,' as in full-bodied with some meat on their bones, or sexy, as in slender or skinny and petite?"

A: "I don't mind kicking it with fine broads or whatever, but petite broads are at the top of my list. If I had to choose between a fine Black broad and a petite chic, the fine one gets kicked to the curb. But that's on a relationship level. On a sex level, if she got that good, it doesn't matter. I can make exceptions if the pussy's good. But petite women are more flexible in bed, and I can have my way with them. I can't fuck her like I want to if she's too thick."

Thaddeus

Q: "Off the top of your head, how would you describe a beautiful, physically attractive Black Woman?"

A: "If she's beautiful, then she's most likely an Alicia Keys in the face, with a body like Rihanna . . . and as ass like Taylor Swift. Ha-ha. Hold up. Scratch Taylor Swift, because she ain't got no ass! But, is she's fair-complexioned, has a nice head of hair, preferably long, and a plump but little enough ass, then I would say she's attractive. Yeah, that's an accurate depiction."

Q: "Physically describe your last three girlfriends. What did they look like?"

A: "My last girlfriend, Elizabeth, is actually white. And the one before her, Julian, was Hispanic. But the three before them were Black—Aisha, Lynn, and Dariana. Aisha and Dariana are light-skinned, and Lynn is light brown. All of them had long hair, pretty faces, small waists, lean bodies or whatever. Aisha has hazel eyes, and Dariana's eyes are kind of light brownish and light greenish. They didn't have too much ass either—just how I like it."

Q: "If you could create your own ideal 'Fantasy Black Woman,' what would she look like?"

A: "She would probably be high yellow [meaning very, very light-skinned], not enough to pass for white, but not the typical-looking Black girl either. Her hair would flow down to her little ass, and she would have a body like the average Victoria's Secret model. And she would have lips like Angelina Jolie, and would be sexy like her too. That would be hot. She'd be an angel without wings."

As you can see, Craig, Kirk, and Thaddeus all prefer Black Women who are considered beautiful by traditional European-American standards, which is evidenced by their responses to the survey questions provided to them. If, for some reason, you disagree with this assertion, let us reflect on some of the things these Black Men said. Here are a few quotes.

Craig: "And her hair has to be at least down to her shoulders. I like it down her back, though, as long as it's straight." "The big booty thing is overrated. I like a woman with a small booty . . ." "Big noses and lips might be the thing in Africa, but not over here in America. I'm Black, but I like Black Women who are pretty in the *American* way."

Kirk: "If I approach a dame and her hair is anything other than straight and well-kept, I'm turning around." "All I date is light-skinned chics. A lot of dark chics are ugly. And the blacker they are, they uglier they are."

Thaddeus: "If she's beautiful, then she's most likely an Alicia Keys in the face, with a body like Rihanna . . . and an ass like Taylor Swift." "They didn't have too much ass either—just how I like it."

Without going into an extensive explication of European-American beauty standards, let me point out what most of us Americans, white *and* Black, already know. Most women in this country who have long hair, small asses, small lips, small noses, and straight hair are white. Women with these features are glorified in the media, especially if they are skinny. So, any other woman, regardless of race, who has those same features, is therefore deemed beautiful. But, if a woman was *not* born this way and modifies herself to *become* such, then something is seriously wrong with this picture. And, because Stupid Black Men do not appreciate their Beautiful Black Women for who they are, large numbers of women in Black communities are striving to become beautiful by standards not of their own. Although, as mentioned earlier, Willie Lynch's brainwashing methods has a lot to do with this, Black Male Stupidity is primarily responsible for Black Men's distorted perceptions of beauty, which cause a lot of problems.

Before we discuss the primary problems caused by Black Men's distorted perceptions of beauty, let me clarify something for the reader. More than anything else, when it comes to beauty, I believe that true beauty is natural and comes in a variety of forms, as opposed to having just one particular standard. All ethnicities have their own standards of beauty, and I respect those standards. But, if a person from one particular ethnicity rejects his or her own standard of beauty, adopts another standard that is not of his or her own, then looks down upon his or her own original standard of beauty as inferior to that of the adopted standard, then I do not respect that. I love women who are not afraid to be who they are.

I have dated and/or had sex with women of *all* races. And one of the most important things I have ever told them is, "Be who you are!" If a woman was Black, I wanted her to be Black. If she was white, I wanted her to be white. The same goes for the Hispanic, Asian, and other women I have been with. I am not impressed by Asian women who want to look non-Asian, Hispanic women who want to look non-Hispanic, white chics who want to look Black, and Black chics who want to look white. I *hate* that! Just be you! If you were born with a big ass, then *love* that big ass! If you were born with a flat ass, then *love* your little pancakes! Recently, a really cool white woman I know told me that her thighs were so sore that she could not bend over pick up anything. I inquired about her soreness, and she said that she had just started a new 60-day workout program called "Brazilian Butt," which, according to her, is supposed to make her butt big. But she does not really have any booty, was not born with any. I then asked her why she joined the program, and this is what she told me: "Well, Cornell, you know, nowadays, white women want Black women's butts, and Black women want white women's butts." I think that is *crazy*. She is beautiful the way she is and should not modify her ass to be accepted as beautiful by others whose beauty standards differ from that of her own. And it is the other way around for Black Women. You all are beautiful just the way you are, so just be yourselves!

Anyway, back to the subject at hand. Stupid Black Men's distorted perceptions of beauty cause some serious problems for Black Women. My focus, however, lies upon what I consider to be the primary problems, of which there are three in total. These problems are listed below.

Problems Caused by Black Men's Distorted Perceptions of Beauty

1. Low self-esteem in Black Women regarding their bodily features, which results in a beauty-related, inferiority complex.
2. Ill-placed pride and self-esteem that results in a beauty-related, superiority complex.
3. Persuasion that causes Black Women to try to change who they are by altering their physical appearances.

Inferiority Complex

A lot of Black Women, misled by Stupid Black Men's distorted perceptions of beauty, begin to lose confidence in their appearances. Among one another, as long as there is no other woman around who is beautiful by traditional European-American standards, they seem confident about the way they look. But put them in a room with a light-skinned, straight haired, petite Black Woman, and watch what happens. Their eyes become shifty, and they become self-conscious, sometimes ill at ease—especially if this other woman's eyes are anything other than just brown or black. The same thing happens when they are not as beautiful as the other woman. In reality, if they were to stick to their own standards of beauty, they would be just as beautiful as the other woman, just by different standards. The reason this is a problem is that, if such Black Women never learn to love the skin that they are in, then they will never truly know self-love. And, without self-love, it will be very hard for them to experience Beautiful *Black* Love.

Superiority Complex

I love ALL of my Beautiful Black Women, but I must keep it real: a lot of my Black Sisters who adhere to European-American beauty standards look down on other Black Women who are comfortable in their own skin and in tune with their Beautiful Blackness. They believe their fair skin and/or straight hair makes them more attractive than other Black Women whose hair is kinky, and whose skin is of a darker shade. These kinds of women are so brainwashed that they do not even know it. In truth, they are not superior at all—they just have an *exaggerated* feeling of being superior to others. And, sometimes, some of these women *do* know that they are not superior, yet they use the illusion of superiority as a psychological defense mechanism in which thoughts and feelings of superiority are used to counter or conceal feelings of inferiority. This not only creates conflict among Black Women, but also intensifies Black Men's distorted perceptions of beauty.

Alteration of Appearance

Believing that they are not beautiful if they do not adhere to European-American standards of beauty, countless Black Women across the country are modifying their appearances to be accepted as beautiful. They perm their hair, use skin bleaching creams, get surgical implants, have plastic surgery, and some even run the risk of having an eating disorder, refusing to eat so that they can become skinny like most of the models on American television. Many wear weaves, while others wear wigs. Some even wear wigs on top of weaves! If a Black Woman is doing this to make a fashion statement, that is okay. But, if she is doing this because she believes it makes her more beautiful than her natural self, then she is undoubtedly brainwashed—mainly because of Stupid Black Men's distorted perceptions.

Anyway, in conclusion, the way that Black Men perceive Black Women tends to influence the way that Black Women perceive themselves. Many Black Men's perceptions of beauty are distorted, which has resulted in many Black Women seeking beauty that is outside of themselves. Such women are victims of Black Male Stupidity. A proper change in Black Men's perceptions can change this.

Chapter Eight

Stupid Black Men's Corruption of Beautiful Black Women

No matter how far I go in life or how much I accomplish, I will *never* forget my experiences in the streets. The crime, poverty, and dereliction that I have witnessed and experienced firsthand will forever be etched into my memory. I often hear people talking about crime and violence in New York, California, and Chicago, but I can attest that the crime in my hometown of New Orleans, Louisiana, is worse. In the other states that I just mentioned, there exists at least some form of solidarity among many of those in the criminal underground, especially with all of the gangs that have been formed there. But, in New Orleans, there are no gangs—it is literally every man for himself. (Let it be stated for the record that when I say "gangs," I am specially referring to large gangs like the Crips, Bloods, Latin Kings, etc., who bind together to participate in widespread criminal activities that occur within a centrally controlled structure.) Criminals in the Big Easy are not too fond of taking orders, so they tend to form *cliques* instead of gangs. I was caught up in the midst of all this. However, in addition to the crime and violence that occurs in New Orleans, one of the things I remember most is the profound mistreatment, degradation, and overall corruption of Black Women. Because of the criminal mentality that is so prevalent there, most Black Women who grow up in urban neighborhoods are viewed by most Black Men growing up in the same neighborhoods as simply tools to be used and abused. These men view Beautiful Black Love as some surreal shit that just happens on TV, or maybe once in a lifetime, and only to certain people. So a lot of my Beautiful Black Sisters down there go through hell while on their quest to find BBL.

In America, wherever there is a ghetto, there is crime, violence, and corruption. And, wherever there are Black Men involved in crime, violence, and corruption, Black Women are oftentimes targeted and/or victimized by the mentality that feeds all of this chaos. So I am dedicating this chapter to Black Women and Men who have lived or still live in urban communities and can directly relate to what I am writing about here. Though Black Men in the ghetto take advantage of women in many ways, my focus in this chapter centers on those who, by way of corruption, turn Black Women into criminals, drug addicts, and/or prostitutes, because I believe that such corruption is one of the stupidest things that Black Men can do to Black Women. All of the incidents I mention here, which you will read about shortly, happened to New Orleanians, because all of the people I surveyed for this chapter are, like me, New Orleans natives. Two of the men that you will read about are longtime career criminals and one is a *former* criminal who changed his life during a decade-plus prison sentence. All of the women you will read about are also former criminals who have changed their lives, and they have one thing in common: they were corrupted into criminality by Black Men they once loved. But, before we get into all of that, let me say a thing or two about some of my experiences regarding criminals, drug addicts, and prostitutes.

In the criminal underworld, there are various levels of criminality. There is crime (misdemeanors), serious crime (non-capital felonies), and *very* serious crime (capital felonies).

In my experience, I have found that Black Men who either commit or are likely to commit serious and very serious crimes are usually more manipulative than those who commit or are likely to commit low-level crimes, especially in their dealings with Black Women. Therefore, the deeper they are into crime, the deeper their manipulation of the Black Woman's mind. My experiences have been drawn from happenings brought about by Black Men who fall into the serious categories of criminality, so I have seen Black Women at their worst.

I know of and have seen Black Women so brainwashed by Black men that not even a bullet to the head, a long stint in prison, or the murders of their own children and families could convince them that the Black Men who put them in all of these situations were not the soul mates they believed them to be. A guy I once knew, who is now deceased, had his girl so strung out on the illusion of love that she left her church-going home just to be with him. Years later, she was so corrupt that she robbed her own family blind to prove her loyalty to him. He eventually went to prison and was later murdered by one of his old enemies after acquiring his freedom. I will not mention their names but, his girl, who is still alive, is currently in a situation in which she is wishing that she were also dead. I have also seen and known other Black Women who, brainwashed by the illusion of Beautiful Black Love, started out selling drugs and ended up being addicted to them. A few of these women have overcome their addictions, but most have not. Some are still addicts on the street, some are addicts in prison, and others have turned to prostitution as a means of acquiring money to support their addictions. A long time ago, all of these Black Women had a lot of potential and probably could have been whatever it was that they wanted to be in life. But Stupid Black Men changed all that. Their lives will never be the same.

Anyway, when I surveyed people for this chapter, in order to provide a balanced view of Black Men's corruption of Black Women, I sought out both Black Men and Women who would tell it like it is. I surveyed men who are still corrupting Black Women's minds to this very day, men who have turned away from such corruption, and women who were once corrupted by men but lived to tell their stories. Six of these surveys remind me of things that I have seen with my own eyes, so I have decided to highlight excerpts from all six of them here in this chapter. These excerpts follow below. As mentioned at the beginning of this book, the names of the people discussed have been changed, their identities withheld. So any resemblance to other persons is thus purely coincidental. Oh, and one more thing. As I also mentioned earlier, because I am not into watering down the truth, I have not omitted any of the expletives used by any of the people mentioned in the following excerpts. Here is what they all had to say about Black Men's corruption of Black Women.

Stanley

Stanley considers himself "a vet in the game," which means that he has been involved in crime for a long time, and this makes him a "veteran." He believes that, in his own words, "real niggas don't change, life is ugly, and every ho has a purpose." He maintains that every woman he becomes intimately involved with is destined to serve him and do whatever he says. If a woman does not follow his orders, he said, then "his pistol will make that ho understand." Here is what else he had to say.

Me: "What's your opinion about Black Men who corrupt the minds of Black Women?"
Stanley: "Like I said a few minutes ago, *every* ho has a purpose. A lot of these bitches just don't realize it until they fuck

with a nigga like me. And almost every ho I got already had the seed of corruption in them when I first met them. They was loving my lifestyle and already knew what they was dealing with when they started fucking with me. Even the so-called innocent ones wasn't all that innocent. So, most of the time, it ain't the nigga corrupting the ho, it's the ho corrupting herself through the nigga. Ya dig? But, even if a nigga *do* corrupt a ho, ain't no rules out there in the streets. It ain't 'bout the ho, it's 'bout *survival*, my nigga."

Me: "When you yourself corrupt women's minds, what kind of things do you make them do?"

Stanley: "All types of shit. But, like I said, it's 'bout survival. So most of the shit I make 'em do deals with my survival. My main bitch, I use her to fish out niggas and set 'em up. She gets rid of my murder weapons. Shit like that. But my other bitch, I got her washing my money. Like I said, every ho got a purpose. If a ho green, give me about eight months, and I'll have the ho all the way out of her mind."

Karl

Karl, like Stanley, is actively involved in crime and does not intend to ever leave the streets.

In fact, when I asked him if he would ever consider relinquishing his criminal lifestyle, his exact response was, "Dawg, the streets *made* me. That's all I know. When I first jumped off the porch [meaning when he first got involved in crime], I know there was no turning back. I'm in it until the death of me." He believes that corruption rules the world and sees nothing wrong with a Black Man corrupting his Black Woman. Here are his responses to the same questions I asked Stanley.

Me: "What's your opinion about Black Men who corrupt the minds of Black Women?"

Karl: "Look around. The world is *full* of corruption. Politicians are corrupt. The police are corrupt. Corruption makes the world go round. Look at the government. They corrupt. They keep talking about the war on drugs, but they keep on letting the drugs come cross the border. Look at the Catholic priests. They so corrupt they fucking *children*. That's just the way of the world, son, human nature. So, if I got to corrupt a bitch to get wherever I need to be in life, then that bitch is getting corrupted. The whole reason I'm ballin' right now is because I got *bitches* pushing my dope. I had to break them in, but they so deep into the game now they ain't trippin'. And all of 'em living good."

Me: "When you yourself corrupt women's minds, what kinds of things do you make them do?"

Karl: "I just make these bitches handle my business. Buy my dope, sell my shit, bring me my money, and I'm good. I'm getting my money right so I can back up out the game. I ain't got no college education or none of that, but these broads do. So I make them use what *they* know while doing what *I* know. It's all about business, so I don't feel sorry for *no* bitch."

Before my interviews with Stanley and Karl, I informed both of them that, because we have totally different lifestyles, I had no desire to maintain communication with them following the interviews. They were cool with that and we went our separate ways immediately after the interviews were over. So I do not know what has become of them. I have not seen either of them on the news, so I assume they are still out there in the streets corrupting the minds of Black Women.

Kenny

Kenny, like me, is a reformed criminal. He had just gotten out of prison when I arranged an interview with him regarding the matter at hand. I am told that he is doing very well now and has a child on the way. He once corrupted Black Women's minds but changed his life while in prison during a decade-plus stint for a violent crime he committed. Here is some of what he had to say about his life regarding female corruption.

Me: "During your days of corruption, in what kinds of ways did you corrupt Black Women's minds?"

Kenny: "My thing was always drug trafficking. I was always moving weight, so I needed people on my team who I could trust. I knew I couldn't really trust none of those other cats, so I brought a lot of women into the fold. On the surface, because I was in college and had two jobs, no one ever thought I was a drug dealer, especially women. So I'd take them out on dates and have sex with them. When I knew I had them, I would ask to use their cars, then secretly load the cars with dope and have them bring gifts to my kids out of town, where the cars would be stolen by my connects. After a few times, I'd tell them what I had been doing, that I would lie and say they were my accomplices if I ever got caught. So, out of fear, they started trafficking the drugs. They ended up liking it—corrupted."

Me: "What made you change your life while you were incarcerated?"

Kenny: "God. I never got caught for drug trafficking or anything drug related, so I knew God had spared my life by giving me a chance to see daylight again after I got convicted for shooting a dude. So I vowed to cherish women when I got out. Plus, I have two daughters. I wouldn't want them to be taken advantage of, so, as a man and as a father, it is my *duty* to change. I'm glad I did. I can rest easy now."

Michelle

Michelle is a former criminal who is now a married mother of two. Here is some of what she had to say about her old life and being corrupted by a Black Man she once loved.

Me: "How did you get involved in crime?"

Michelle: "I was misled by what I thought was love. My ex, Eugene, broke me in when I was 14 years old. I knew he was in the streets, and I thought I could change him, but I couldn't. He wanted me to prove my loyalty to him by shooting another female, and I was so in love with him I did it. I did seven years on that, and he abandoned me after I got convicted. That's when I realized I had to do something with myself. It's sad that he took advantage of my young mind like that, but I've learned from it."

Toya

Toya, like Michelle, is a former criminal who was corrupted by a Black Man but changed her life while in prison. Here is some of what she had to say in response to the same question.

Me: "How did you get involved in crime?"

Toya: "I was already committing crimes as a teenager, but it was just petty crimes like shoplifting and boosting jewelry. But I didn't get into *serious* crime until I met Jarnell, my son's daddy. He's in jail now, doing life. He had me fooled, thinking he loved me. But I was just a stepping stone to him. I handled his drugs and his money. But one day he convinced me to sleep with his enemy so he could kill him while I was in bed with him. Anyway, he shot the dude that night, but the dude lived and snitched to the police. But, somehow, from jail he was able to convince the dude to say *I'm* the one who shot him. So I went to jail on attempted murder. He tried to write me a few times when I was in jail, but I never read his letters. I'll *never* forgive him for what he did to me. I lost a lot of years of my life in that place. He's wrong for that."

Ebony

Ebony's situation, compared to that of Michelle and Toya, was the worst. She has been in and out of jail numerous times but eventually changed her life. Here is some of what she had to say.

Me: "Tell me about your situation regarding a Black Man corrupting your mind. What happened?"

Ebony: "It wasn't just *one* Black Man—It was *a lot* of them. I was really gullible in my youth, always seeking validation from men, so they took advantage of that. They made me think it was okay to have sex with various men and do drugs, and I got addicted to both. But when I went to jail for, like, the fifth time, I started writing different guys who were also in jail, and this is when I met Andre. I was desperate and fell in love with him through the mail. We got out around the same time, had a lot of sex, did a lot of drugs together, and I got strung out on heroin. He was my provider, but he went back to jail, and we stayed in contact by phone and mail. He persuaded me to have sex with other drug dealers to support my addiction, and I was so confused I took his advice. Three years later, I was out on corners selling my body just to get a fix. I was in and out of jail for prostitution. When one of my friends got raped and killed, I knew it was time to walk away from all that. It wasn't easy, and it took a while, but I did it. Six months later, I was diagnosed with HIV. The only thing on my mind is God and living and dying happy. I haven't found love yet, but I'm happy, despite how my life turned out."

Black Women like Michelle, Toya, and Ebony are oftentimes overlooked by people who do studies on Black Women. The reason is that no one really cares about women who are or once was involved in a life of crime. But these women got put through the ringer by men, so I wanted to highlight them here to somewhat educate the public about what they go through. The Black Men who put them through what they went through were stupid, because real men do not corrupt the minds of their women. They love them too much to do so. When I think about men like Stanley, Karl, and Kenny, my heart goes out to all of the Black Women who are and have been victimized by these men's corruptive mentalities. When a Black Man corrupts his woman's mind, he causes her all kinds of problems, especially if the corruption leads to crime, drug addiction, and prostitution.

When a Black Woman is turned into a criminal, not only does this remove a nurturer from a Black home, but it also worsens the plight of the Black Woman, not to mention utterly destroys her whole life. Any child that she gives birth to will most likely be born into corruption and grow up to become an additional link of the chain of ignorance found in corrupted Black communities. The mother of that child lives a useless life because she is not contributing anything meaningful to our society. The same goes for Black Women who are turned into drug addicts and prostitutes. Drugs destroy the mind and prostitution heightens the spread of sexually transmitted diseases. Once the mind is destroyed, the body that carries that mind is simply a waste of both a body *and* mind. And the spreading of STDs only kills us Black people off. Therefore, unless such a woman finds within herself the strength to relinquish her life of crime, overcome her drug addiction, and/or give up her life of prostitution, only suffering, incarceration, and death will await her. She will never truly experience the magical feeling of Beautiful Black Love. Black Men need to cogitate this before they consider corrupting their Black Women's minds. By corrupting our Beautiful Black Women, we are only throwing ourselves and BBL into the fires of extinction.

Chapter Nine

Black Men's Inconsiderate Neglect of Black Women

In the Author's Note at the beginning of this book, I mentioned that some people, while reading this book, may assume that I oppose interracial relationships. I was alluding to this chapter, because it discusses how many Black Men neglect Black Women for non-Black women, just for the hell of it. Well, I would like to clarify, once more, at the outset of this chapter that I am NOT opposed to interracial relationships because, as I also stated in the Author's Note, I am not so naïve to believe that love is confined by race. Love does not come in colors, and no race of people anywhere upon the face of the earth has a monopoly on love. So my beef is not with Black Men or Black Women who happen to fall in love outside of the Black world—it is with Stupid Black Men who, having no real interest in long-lasting interracial relationships, neglect Black Women for non-Black women for no real reason at all.

Let me give you an example of what I am talking about. I have a white homeboy named Christopher Pelican. We became close during our years together in college and on the job as librarians. Pelican loves *all* women—especially Black Women. He sincerely believes that Black Women are some of the most beautiful creatures on earth, and he is absolutely down for being in a long-lasting relationship with a Black Woman. I sincerely know in my heart that he can make some Black Woman out there happy for all eternity. But I also have an associate, whose name

I will not mention, who is Black and says that he would never marry a white woman—unless she is rich—because he claims to have no interest whatsoever in interracial relationships. Yet, every time he sees a white woman he deems attractive, he goes crazy with lust. But he does not go similarly crazy upon seeing Beautiful Black Women who are just as or even more attractive. I recently talked to him about all of this and the following is what he told me: "There's just something about these white girls, man. I want to fuck them, but I don't want to *be* with them. But *Black* Women, I want to be with them, and I also want to fuck them, but not as much as I want to fuck these white girls. So I fuck these white girls and then go back to the Black ones when I burn out on all the white ones."

Like I told my associate, not only does this shit sound stupid, but also it is unfair to both the white *and* Black Women. The reason is that the Black Women are being looked over simply so that he can treat the white women like sex slaves. If the white women fall in love with him, their hearts get broken. The same goes for the Black Women. He is not driven by love but by lust, which makes him stupid, because he also told me that he "has love for *all* women." He is confused. Therefore, it is people like him that I am talking about in this chapter. With that said, this section, as you now see, is not about interracial relationships, but rather Stupid Black Men who look over their own women because they are driven by lust instead of love. This is what this chapter is *really* about.

Anyway, there are a lot of Black Men like my associate. Most of them seem to be young, but there are definitely some older ones, too. When I set out to survey Black Men for this chapter, I initially believed that I would have to search high and low to find Black Men who were willing to keep it real about why they neglect their Beautiful Black Women in the ways that they do. But I was wrong. Black Men *flooded* me with information regarding this topic, and I have found that, according to what the majority of them told me, lust is what drives them to seek out non-Black women. Most of them prefer white women, but Hispanic women are the second preference, and Asian women are the third. And most of those men said that, because they still desire Black Women, they do not believe their strong disregard for Black Women is a form of neglect. Here are a few excerpts from my interviews with some of these men. Check out their stupidity.

Damon

Damon is a 34-year-old Black man who says he loves his Beautiful Black Women, but "they are the reason he pursues non-Black women." He fails to take responsibility for his own actions.

Me: "What motivates you to choose non-Black women over Black Women?"

Damon: "I just started dating outside my race after my honorable discharge from the Army. Before that, I was always dating or in and out of relationships with Black Women. Truth is, I have a strong sex drive, so, no matter how nice or sweet or strong a woman is, if she can't please me sexually, we won't last. Black women are too inhibited in the bedroom, scared to do this, and scared to do that. So, when I went overseas to places like Italy, France, Brazil, and lots of other places like Tokyo, and I saw how uninhibited the women were, this broadened my options. So, when I came back to the states, I started dating every non-Black woman I could find. Out of all of them, the white girls were the most uninhibited, so I kind of got hooked on them. They'll do almost *anything* in bed, so they satisfy my sexual appetite. But it's all about sex, though. I'm not trying to settle down with any of them. I'll do that with a Black Woman, if I can find the right one."

Me: "Do you have any genuine interest in interracial relationships? I know you just said that you're not trying to or don't plan to settle down with any white girls, but I'm curious and want to know if you'd consider settling down with any other non-Black woman."

Damon: "I'm not really into the interracial thing. I'm not racist, but I just can't imagine me living out the rest of my life with anything other than a Black Woman. It's just hard to find the right Black Woman who can satisfy me in bed and on a lot of other levels. So, until I find one, I'm going to keep dating these non-Black bombshells. I don't date for love—I date for sex."

Me: "Do you ever feel like you're neglecting Black Women by dating how you date?"

Damon: "No, because, like I just told you, I'm just broadening my options. Besides, it's not like I'm *not* dating Black Women, because I still date some of them too. I just date more non-Black than Black. But it's *their* fault, anyway. If they were willing to do what all these non-Black women do, then I wouldn't have to look beyond them for anything or anybody. Black Women have too many issues, especially when it comes to sex."

Latarius

Latarius is a 26-year-old college student who refused to attend historically Black colleges and universities because he believes that "all of the pro-Black stuff on campus would've limited the amount of non-Black pussy he could've gotten." So now he attends a primarily white college. Here is some of what he had to say in response to the same questions I asked Damon.

> Me: "What motivates you to choose non-Black women over Black Women?"
>
> Latarius: "The reason I'm so light-skinned is because most of my immediate family is mixed. My mom is half Black and half white, and my dad is half Black and half Hispanic. So I grew up having all kinds of girlfriends. I've never been into the pro-Black thing like my mom and dad. They always told me to be colorblind, but they also only wanted me to have a Black wife when I grew up. They wanted me to go to a Black college. But I don't think inside of the color box. But I tried the Black Woman thing a couple of times, and I always got disappointed by how limited their minds are in comparison to other women from other cultures. And sex with other women is almost always better, so I just go where the best is. My parents don't like it, but they'll get over it."

> Me: "Are you genuinely interested in interracial relationships, or is it just all about the sex?"

> Latarius: "I guess you can say that sometimes I'm interested in interracial relationships, like, if I meet a non-Black woman I really like. But, when I really think about it, it's mostly just about the sex. I say that because, at the college I attend, which is mostly white, all the white girls *love* me. I fuck so many of them I lose count, and I never even considered having a relationship with any of them. I once dated a Black chic there, but she was looking for

a man, and I wasn't ready for all that. And the white girls were more fun, so I dumped her and went back to the white girls."

Me: "How does neglecting Black Women make you feel?"

Latarius: "I don't think I'm neglecting them. Neglecting them would be like not giving them the time of day. They need to step their game up, because they're so far behind all the other women, especially the white girls. I remember one time I asked this Black girl I was sleeping with to give me head, and she refused, even though I was performing oral sex on her. But I don't even have to *ask* these white girls. They just pull my shit out and start sucking it!"

Verone

Verone is 24 years of age and is one of those young Black Men who are caught up into the hip-hop/swagger phenomenon. He believes that "Black pussy is good but it's getting played out." Here is some of what he had to say.

Me: "When it comes to relationships, what kind of women do you prefer?"

Verone: (Laughs) "Relationships? Kid, I'm 24. *Fuck* a relationship! I'm a young diver getting my dick wet. I'm all about getting *pussy*, and I *rank* my pussy. Latina pussy is first, Asian pussy is second, white pussy is third, Black pussy is fourth, and other pussy is last. If I ever wife a damsel, though, she ain't gonna be Black, because Black Women are getting played out. That's why Ice T got Coco. Ditty had J-Lo. And even a lot of Black Women know they are getting played out. That's why you see so many of them dating white boys. Halle Berry likes white boys."

Me: "What gives you the impression that Black Women are played out?"

Verone: "It's all over the media, Black dudes leaving Black Women for women who are *not* Black, especially leaving them for white girls. I was just reading some shit on the Internet about Jesse Jackson's son, Congressman Jesse Jackson Jr. He talks all that Black shit but just got caught having an affair with a white woman, a blond DC hostess. Look at all the white bitches Tiger Woods got caught cheating with. And Herman Cain sold his wife out for a white woman. You *know* that white pussy fire if it makes you lose your chance at becoming President of the United States! Black Men just don't want Black Women no more. They're just washed up now. And these Latinas and Asian women are taking over. That's why I'm learning Spanish and Mandarin Chinese on Rosetta Stone."

Me: "Do you ever feel guilty about neglecting your Beautiful Black Women?"

Verone: "Homie, I did two years in jail. And, when I was in, all the Black Women I had before I got locked up forgot about me. And all the Black Women I tried to get hooked up with thought they was too much to write a nigga in jail. I didn't complain, though, when they neglected me. They didn't care, so I didn't care. Revenge is a motherfucker!"

Eddie

Eddie is a 50-year-old Black Man who is married to a Hispanic woman. Like me, in addition to English, he speaks Spanish. So he requested that our interview be fully and completely conducted in Spanish. However, because most of my readers speak English, I have translated the following excerpt into English from Spanish.

Me: "Why did you marry a Hispanic woman?"

Eddie: "Well, actually, at first, we never intended to get married. Our relationship was based mainly on sex, because we both were in troubled relationships at the time. I had a crazy Black girlfriend who always wanted to fuss and fight, and she had a Latino boyfriend who acted the same way. I was tired of Black Women, she was tired of Latino men, so we left the person we had and ran away together. We got married and have been happy together ever since. We have a nice bilingual family now."

Me: "How did your experience with the crazy Black girlfriend affect your overall perception of Black Women?"

Eddie: "Really, it didn't affect my perception. It just proved what I had already known: Black Women are crazy! My mother and all her sisters were the same way. All of my female cousins, too. So I was just tired of being around all of that craziness. I was looking for a way out, and I found it through my wife."

Me: "So, you believe that all Black Women are crazy?"

Eddie: "The Black American ones. Black Hispanic women are different, because the Hispanic culture is different. Hispanic women are loyal and respectful, but Black American women have no true values."

Me: "Hypothetically speaking, if your wife and you were to divorce, what kind of women would you date?"

Eddie: "Spanish-speaking women. I don't ever want to experience all of that crazy behavior with a Black Woman again. I'm a part of Hispanic culture now, and my wife is beautiful inside and out. She keeps me happy. I feel like I'm 25 again. If I were married to a Black Woman, I would probably feel twice my age or be dead from all the stress she put me through."

There are a lot of Black Men out there like Damon, Latarius, Verone, and Eddie, all of whom find absolutely nothing wrong with neglecting Black Women for non-Black women without any real interest in interracial relationships. Younger Black Men like Damon, Latarius and Verone outnumber older guys like Eddie, but I included Eddie's story because his situation reflects that of many other Black Men his age who end up married to, or simply in intimate relationships with, non-Black women. In the beginning, their dealings with these women are usually just based on sex. They do not consider anything long-lasting until failed relationships with Black Women cause them to do a sort of compare and contrast between Black and non-Black women, and their bitterness regarding the failed relationships pushes them further in the direction of the non-Black women they get intimately involved with. And, because so many Black Men are looking over their own women for non-Black women, especially for sexual reasons, this causes serious problems for the Black Women in America.

Problems Caused by Black Woman Neglect

When Beautiful Black Women are neglected by their own men, all of the following problems arise:

1. Black Women, who are already discriminated against because of both their gender and skin color, feel unwanted and sometimes give up on Beautiful Black Love.
2. Black Women grow bitter toward Black men, and this bitterness destroys their future relationships with other Black Men.
3. Racist people in society use Black Men's neglect of their own women to justify their belief that Black Women are inferior, which only creates more and more problems for Black Women.
4. Black Men eventually brainwash themselves into believing that their own women are inferior to non-Black women.

The Feeling of Being Unwanted

The feeling of being unwanted is one of the worst feelings a woman could ever experience, because it is part of a woman's nature to want to be wanted by her man. And a lot of Black Women in this country are constantly encountering people who view them as if they are worthless. So, the desire of their men is crucial to the development of their self-esteem. When a Black Man turns a blind eye to his own woman but lay his eyes upon another, his woman is left in a state of despair. "Why does he not desire me but desire her?" she wonders. "Is there something wrong with me?" The Black Man she loves never really gives her any answers, so she usually gives up on both him and the Beautiful Black Love she once believed in. This lessens her chances of finding true love with her Black mate, because she runs away from love.

Bitterness

Some Black Women never get over the neglected actions carried out by the Black Men they either loved or wanted so desperately to love. As the old street saying goes, they "feel played." So they become unforgiving. As a consequence, they take their anger out on many of the Black Men they later get involved with. They displace that anger, and this only runs Black Men away. So their relationships fail, and they eventually end up more bitter than they were before.

Justification of Racism

Racist people are so brainwashed by their own ignorance that they will use almost *anything* as proof to justify what they believe. So, when racist people who believe that Black Women are inferior see Black Men looking over their own women, they are further convinced that they were right all along. And this feeling of justification only leads to more discrimination and ill treatment of Black Women by racist, non-Black parties in everything from the workforce to day-to-day life in our society.

Self-Brainwashing of Black Men

It is a fact that anything a person does long enough becomes a habit. So, when Black Men constantly tell themselves and others that non-Black women are better than Black Women at this and that, eventually, they begin viewing Black Women as inferior to non-Black women. And, when this happens, the possibility of

Beautiful Black Love being shared between these men and their potential Black mates is destroyed.

Anyway, thus far, all of the chapters you have read highlight Black Male Stupidity. Let us now turn our discussion over to the subject of Beautiful Black Love.

PART 2

BEAUTIFUL BLACK LOVE

Chapter Ten

Beautiful Black Love Acceptance

E arlier in this book, I opened Chapter One with discussion of unfaithfulness, betrayal, misguided ideology and belief modification. Because the bulk of that chapter was centered on unfaithfulness, betrayal, and misguided ideology, however, I have yet to expound on the subject of belief modification. Therefore, before we enter discussion regarding Beautiful Black Love acceptance, let me say a thing or two about modification of belief as it concerns the subject of BBL.

When it comes to the human mind, whatever one believes is one's reality. One can profess to be a Christian, for example, but if this person believes that wealth accumulation is more important than, say, Jesus Christ, then he or she, because of this belief, is not really a Christian. Why? Because Christians are supposed to put God first, not money. Thus, putting money first makes such a person un-Christian. In the same way, if a person believes that Beautiful Black Love is only a thing of fantasy, or that other things are more important than Beautiful Black Love, then, until this person changes his or her belief, he or she will never find Beautiful Black Love. To the former, "money rules" is his or her reality. To the latter, "Beautiful Black Love is insignificant" is also a reality. And, until these beliefs change, nothing or no one will be able to convince such people otherwise.

Now, in the first part of this book, we have discussed Black Male Stupidity on nine different levels. What this has taught us is that, at the very least, there are nine beliefs that hinder Black Men from discovering Beautiful Black Love. So, in order to change Stupid Black Men, we need not focus on trying to change the individual man—we need to modify his beliefs. The only way that we can do this is by collectively incorporating Beautiful Black Love into all of the things that *influence* his beliefs. This brings us to the following question: What influences Black Men's beliefs?

Primarily, Black Men acquire most of their beliefs during their childhood years, so parental figures and role models are their first true forms of influence. These beliefs serve as the basis of what they do and why they do it. But, as they get older, society becomes their second form of influence. Since we cannot turn back the hands of time and modify Black Men's upbringings, our only option is to modify their beliefs through social influence. This brings us to the second question: How can we modify Black Men's beliefs through social influence?

The power of social influence lies in the various means of mass communication that we think of as a whole, which we call the "mass media," and consists of television, newspapers, radio, and the Internet. If Black people in America who have access to these means bombard the public with images of Beautiful Black Love, then, eventually, Black Men's beliefs will change. Look at what happened during the Black Power movement in the United States in the 1960s. When Black People united and began expressing a new racial consciousness, and they started bombarding the public with images of Black Power, Black people all over the nation and the world, many of whom previously did not believe that Black Power was all that powerful, began modifying their beliefs about Black Power. In seemingly no time at all, Black People who were once disrespectful to each other were respecting each other! Black leaders began popping up from out of nowhere. Black pride was seen almost *everywhere*! Black Women were respected and treated like goddesses. So just imagine what would happen if we put the same energy and momentum behind a Beautiful Black Love movement.

I was watching Viola Davis on television several weeks ago, and she said that most of the scripts she receives from young black screenwriters aim to cast her in stereotypical, crack head-like roles. But just imagine what would happen if these young screenwriters were to start writing new screenplays depicting Beautiful Black Love. I look through book catalogs and see a million and one urban novels celebrating life in the ghetto. Imagine what would happen if the authors of all these novels start writing bestselling books about Beautiful Black Love. What if my Beautiful Black Brothers Spike Lee and Tyler Perry put their differences aside and start collaborating on movie projects depicting Beautiful Black Love? What if a lot of influential rappers were to stop degrading Black Women in their songs and videos and start rapping about Beautiful Black Love, while staying true to their core audiences? What if Oprah had a show about Beautiful Black Love broadcast on her OWN network? Do you see where I'm going with this? All of this BBL depiction would positively influence public perception and, in the process, Black Men's beliefs would change. Of course, *all* Black Men would not be saved, but many of them would be. However, they will not begin to accept the notion of BBL until large numbers of us Black people come together and give them a *reason* to want to accept it. This is just how we operate as a people. A lot of Black Men in America did not believe that a man of African descent in this day and age would ever become President of the United States—until we came together and *gave* them a reason to believe. And look at Obama now. So Black

Men's beliefs *can* change. They just need a Beautiful Black Love campaign. Whenever a large enough one arises, Black Men's perceptions *will* change. Believe it!

Anyway, with all of that said, let us now officially move on to the subject of BBL acceptance.

Beautiful Black Love Acceptance

When we Black people stop running away from Beautiful Black Love and start embracing it, everything that we think we know about love changes, and we wonder to ourselves, "Why in the hell didn't I give in to love earlier?" I swear, it feels so *good*! Beautiful Black Love is so special, so sweet, so otherworldly that it makes one *know* that nothing else really matters. Because God is Love and Woman is Goddess, it deepens our relationship with, and our connection to, both. As I stated in the Foretroduction, BBL is so potent that it cannot be described. It can only be seen and felt. So, as I also did in the Foretroduction, I would like to refer to true Black marital relationships that I believe paint a clear picture of what I mean when I mention Beautiful Black Love. These relationships are as follows:

1. Coretta Scott and Martin Luther King's marriage.
2. Betty and Malcolm Shabazz's marital relationships.
3. Michelle and Barack Obama's marital union.
4. Jada Pinkett and Will Smith's matrimony.
5. Serita and T.D. Jakes' marriage.

One need not even know any of these people personally, because Beautiful Black Love tells all and does not lie. One can simply look at television footage of them and see BBL in its state of effervescence. But here is why I believe that all of these people's relationships are examples of Beautiful Black Love.

Coretta Scott and Dr. Martin Luther King

Considering all of the things Martin and Coretta had to go through during the Civil Rights era—racism, incarceration, the threat of infidelity and divorce, and much more—it is obvious that Beautiful Black Love is what kept these two together. Coretta seemed to always be standing right beside her husband, during both the good and the bad times. And they looked happy together, as if not even death could end their love. They remained devoted to each other during this pivotal point in their lives. And Coretta was so steadfastly loyal to King that, whereas most other Black Women would have run for the hills in fear, she joined him in civil rights demonstrations. After King's assassination, Coretta continued to lead major demonstrations, organized marches to promote King's principles, and succeeded at her campaign to establish a national holiday honoring her great husband. She represented her man until her own death, not simply because she was a good wife, but because she was driven by Beautiful Black Love until the Reaper came for her soul.

I remember reading about something else that deepened my respect for Coretta and Dr. King. Once, while perusing some stuff on *Encarta Reference Library Premium 2005,* I came across something I believe was entitled "Interview with Spike Lee." Well, in the interview, I remember reading something about how J. Edgar Hoover had tapes made of King with other women. The tapes were used for blackmail-like purposes. King was told that, if he did not commit suicide, the tapes would be sent to Coretta. Well, King refused to commit suicide, and the tapes were sent to Coretta. If my memory serves me correctly and all of this is true, the sheer fact that Coretta stayed with King, and King took responsibility for his actions instead of chickening out and just killing himself, proves that these two partners believed in Beautiful Black Love, knowing that it would get them through all of the chaos. Moreover, the fact that Hoover would even *do* such a thing proves that even King's enemies could see how strong King and Coretta's love was. If Beautiful Black Love was not involved, then Coretta would have left King a long time ago—but she never did.

Betty and Malcolm Shabazz

In many ways, Betty and Malcolm X's marriage was similar to that of Coretta's and King's, minus the infidelity. Like King, Malcolm was a powerful man who was faced with the threat of racism, incarceration, and death, but none of these things could ever destroy the Beautiful Black Love Malcolm and Betty shared. They also looked happy when they were together. And, because Malcolm was considered a militant leader, the threats that he and Betty faced were oftentimes worse than those that King and Coretta faced. They loved each other through it all. Betty was a dutiful Muslim wife. Like all couples, they had a few problems. She even left him temporarily on several occasions, but BBL always brought her back to him. After Malcolm's assassination, Betty never stopped loving him and even helped him become a cultural hero. If she were still alive, I would hug that woman so lovingly and tell her in a million ways how much I love and respect her for staying true to Malcolm as best as she could. Sadly, however, after receiving third degree burns over 95 percent of her body in a fire set by her own grandson, she died. But the Beautiful Black Love that she and Malcolm shared will *never* be forgotten.

Michelle and Barack Obama

Because Barack and Michelle are always at the forefront of the mass media, I will not go into detail about their wonderful marital history together. I will assume that you have already seen their Beautiful Black Love in action while watching them on television. I see passionate love oozing from each of them every time I see them together on TV. In fact, even when one of them is seen on television without the other but *mentioning* the other, the same passionate love can be seen clearly. I was recently watching Michelle on TV, on one of those late night talk shows (I cannot remember which show it was, but on it she swapped food with the talk show host, and they, Michelle and the host, ate), and every time Michelle mentioned Barack's name and talked about him, I could literally *feel* her love for him. And this is how I know that the BBL shared between them is one hundred percent real on both ends.

Will and Jada Pinkett-Smith

I have never really researched Will and Jada's marital relationship because, every time I see them together on television or in magazines, I can also feel the love shared between them. So I do not feel the need to do any research—my eyes see it all. Now, I am told, and I remember reading somewhere, that they have an open relationship. If this is true, then I respect them even more because only Beautiful Black Love can keep people in their position together. I also remember reading about some rumors regarding them supposedly getting divorced but, as far as I know, they are still together at the time of this writing, which means that BBL is still keeping them close to each other. I saw them together in a magazine again recently, and I still felt BBL oozing from them, so I know their love is real. The fact that it can be felt so many miles away from someone they do not even know is proof of this.

Serita and T.D. Jakes

I have always been hearing nice things about Bishop T.D. Jakes, but I had never heard anything about his wife, Serita, until the end of 2011 when I picked up a November 2011 issue of *Sister 2 Sister* magazine. On page 76 of this issue, there is an in-depth interview about Serita and her husband that was conducted by Jamie Foster Brown, the magazine's publisher. I had chills all over my body while reading this interview because I could feel the Beautiful Black Love that Serita shares with her husband. I urge all of my readers to not only order this back issue of *Sister 2 Sister* and read this article, but also subscribe to the magazine because Jamie, who has been married for over 40 years, knows what she is talking about when she talks about love.

Anyway, Serita and Bishop, at the time of this writing, have been married for almost 30 years. Bishop is one of the most powerful preachers in America, but their love has been real since the beginning, since Bishop was powerless. Before all of their success, Bishop worked at a chemical plant, but he lost his job, and his unemployment funds ran out. So Serita found employment as a Christian radio station DJ and warehouse supervisor to support her hubby, who stayed at home and cut grass. They even went without utilities once, with no phone, no water, and no power—but Serita stuck by him. They once got into a car accident and, when Serita could not walk, the Bishop stayed home for an entire year helping her until she could walk again. And, in all of their years of marriage, they have had about less than five arguments. In addition, when women use trickery in their attempts to try to steal her man, Serita trusts Bishop, knows that he will not cheat on her. And Serita loves Bishop so much that she "wants what is best for him, even if it is not her." It is examples like this that prove that what Serita and T.D. Jakes share is undoubtedly Beautiful Black Love.

Imagine what love would be like in the Black world if more Black couples were to share the same kind of Beautiful Black Love that all of the above-mentioned couples share. What if more of our Black Men were as serious as Martin Luther King Jr., Malcolm X, Barack Obama, Will Smith, and T.D. Jakes? Today, our world would be a better place. There are several lessons that can be learned from all of the above-mentioned relationships.

The first lesson is that Beautiful Black Love is so powerful that things like racism, incarceration, and the threat of infidelity, or even death, cannot destroy it. The second lesson is that, even in the midst of breakups, Beautiful Black Love will draw partners together. The third lesson is that BBL is not only seen but also felt by the partners in love as well as everybody else, even when the partners are not in each other's presence. And the fourth and final lesson is that Beautiful Black Love is as strong in prosperity as it is in prosperity's absence. All of these lessons mean that there is nothing, no force whatsoever upon the face of this earth or anywhere in the universe, that can stop the power of or put an end to Beautiful Black Love. As I said earlier, God is Love. Because of this, and because we people of African descent were the first humans created upon the earth, if we open ourselves to the notion and reality of Beautiful Black Love, then we can and will experience BBL in its purest form. All we have to do is accept it. Only then can we reap the rewards that Beautiful Black Love has to offer. Black Men need to realize that there are benefits of BBL acceptance.

The Benefits of BBL Acceptance

The first primary benefit of Beautiful Black Love acceptance is positive life change by way of belief modification. When one embraces the idea of BBL, all of the old, negative beliefs he or she held lose all of their power to the strength of the new belief held about BBL. Therefore, one's perception changes and, because one's perception is one's reality, and one's reality dictate how one lives his or her life, BBL acceptance creates positive change in one's experience.

The second benefit of BBL acceptance is appreciation of life and love. After one's misguided beliefs are modified and his or her life is positively changed by BBL acceptance, one feels appreciative of life and love, so much so that one sees nothing but love inside of everything that has the breath of life within it. The whole world, in spite of its imperfection, becomes beautiful. Love, in all of its greatness, is respected to the fullest. One comes to the realization that, on earth, life and love are the most powerful forces known to mankind. So he or she respects that.

The third benefit is supreme happiness by way of eradication of stress. See, when one appreciates life and love, stress, which is usually the result of *discontent* with life and love, goes away. And the absence of stress opens the door to happiness. Once one walks through that door, the feeling of happiness becomes addictive, compelling one to constantly pursue it. The more one pursues and feels happiness, the happier one becomes. Therefore, the feeling of happiness becomes increasingly intensified—supreme.

The fourth and final benefit of BBL acceptance is the creation of change by way of inspiration. When one is happy because he or she appreciates life and love, then everyone who is praying attention sees BBL oozing from this person. And those observing this, if in lack of such love, then aspire to acquire the same feeling. BBL becomes contagious. Thus, as BBL is sought and experienced by the newly inspired person, change begins taking place in the inspired person's heart. This internal change leads to external change, this external change begins modifying beliefs, and this cycle of BBL acceptance/benefits starts all over again.

Truly, Beautiful Black Love is *powerful*. Once we embrace it, believe me, *anything* is possible.

Chapter Eleven

The Loving Nature
of the Black Woman

It is easy to understand the Black Woman if one just pays attention. We can sum her up with only one word: Love. This is because everything that she does, in one way or another, is somehow connected to love. Love is just the Black Woman's nature. This is what makes her so beautiful, why she is so precious, why I love her so much! If you, the reader, are a man, think of all the Black Women you know, the good ones and the bad ones. What makes them good? What makes them bad? The answers to these questions are somehow connected to love.

Good Black Women are good because, at some time in their lives, they experienced pleasurable love in some kind of form, and this love rubbed off on them so much that they began acting in a loving way, doing loving things. The love they encountered may have come from their parents or other parental figures, loving role models or friends, or even loving partners with whom they shared a loving bond. In contrast, bad Black women are bad because, at some time in *their* lives, they experienced the *absence* of love in some kind of form, and this lack of love affected them so much that they began acting and behaving in unloving ways, doing unloving things. The lack of love they encountered may have also come from their parents or parental figures, old intimate partners, or others.

Beyond such a limited scope, though, Black Women, like all other women, are *born* into this earth realm to love and to nurture, which is why they, not men, were created by God with the biological blessing we call the "womb." Whole nations spring forth from women's wombs, and it is the love and nurturing provided by women that allow these nations to grow into nations before they, these nations, are even cognizant of what the word "nation" means. But what makes the *Black* Woman so special is that, long before there were any other feminine human beings upon the earth, there was the Black Woman. Instead of just giving birth to whole nations, she has given birth to the whole of humanity. And, wherever Black Women are found, love is found. Wherever a Black Woman's love is found, nurturing is found. So, whenever an unloving, un-nurturing Black Woman is found, one needs to realize that she is *not* the way she is because such is her nature—she is the way she is because her loving and nurturing nature has been taken for granted. When people in general, particularly Black Men, begin to realize this, the Beautiful Black Woman will be seen in all of her natural, loving beauty.

When it comes to the subject of Black Women, I cannot really hold any real conversations with many other men, because we are usually not on the same level regarding this. They have been trained to take Black Women at face value, but I am intelligent enough to know that, where people are concerned in general, a person is not usually the person he or she seems to be on the surface. Therefore, whereas most other Black Men see Black Women as stuck up, crazy, and/or evil or whatever, I simply see them as naturally beautiful creatures that protect themselves by way of defense mechanisms to avoid being hurt again. Consequently, when I encounter so-called "bad" Black Women with messed up attitudes, I am never really turned off or put off by their antics. In fact, I usually deem it a challenge to see how long it takes to make such women smile. Unless they are just too far gone and corrupt or whatever, most Black Women, despite how much they may try to hide or deny it, are really sweet underneath the facades they create. There is no way that they can eradicate this from their nature.

As I am writing this, three particular Black Women I know come to mind. All of them hold job positions that give them authority over men, and they are all considered "stuck up" by most of the men around them. The first woman is a beautiful dark-skinned Sister that I met about two years ago through an associate of mine who was a friend of hers. I was in college at the time, acing all my exams, as usual. One day, this woman told my associate that she had made the Dean's list in college. My associate then told her that I always made the Chancellor's list, which is above the Dean's. They started playfully debating about who was the smarter one—her or me? Eventually, a meeting was arranged between this woman and me, and we engaged in some nice conversation. I read some of her college essays. She read the opening chapters of one of my manuscripts. She was really cool. Not once did she act stuck up with me, but I have witnessed her going into stuck up mode with other men. What makes me so different? She saw for herself that I was and am not like any of those other men. She knew that I was and am an intelligent, handsome, fine Black Man who loves, adores, respects, and cherishes Black Women. I could see the loving nature inside of her, yearning to escape. I have not seen her in quite some time, but when I do see her on rare occasions, I see not a stuck up Black Woman but a gorgeous, dark-skinned goddess whose beauty and loving nature reigns supreme.

The second woman is an older woman who pretends to be mean but is, beneath the surface, so sweet that she would probably buckle at the knees if I were to kiss her lips, especially give her a little tongue! Almost every guy I meet who knows her says that she is crazy in addition to other bad things about her. But she has never treated me in any mean or disrespectful way during any of my encounters with her. Anyway, I once did a little research about her and discovered that, a long time ago, she fell deeply in love with a guy who broke her heart and stole some of her personal belongings when he became addicted to drugs. Well, ever since then, she has been putting on an illusory mask of meanness whenever she encounters men who somehow remind her of the man who broke her heart. I must not remind her of him. I remember making her smile and laugh once, for only a brief moment, and she had one of the most beautiful smiles that I have ever seen. I see Black elegance and love whenever I see her. Underneath it all, she is really a good, loving Black Woman.

The third woman is also an older woman, one who is very attractive and turns heads everywhere she goes. Many people say that she is a lesbian, but I do not know for sure if this is true, because I have never seen her doing anything lesbian-like. If she *is* lesbian, though, she is one *fine* ass lesbian! But, I am willing to bet that, prior to lesbianism, she gave her heart away to some Stupid Black Man who broke it in pieces. Anyway, this Sister is one of those bossy, professional types who is not afraid to let men know that she is the one running things. Most of the guys I know who have encountered her say she is a stuck up, power hungry, manhating bitch. I do not see it that way. Whenever I envision her, I see her as a strong Black Woman who has worked hard to get where she is in this male chauvinistic world, a Black Woman whose loving nature is, like the second woman's, oftentimes hidden beneath a created exterior. Another thing I like about her is that, from what I have seen with my own eyes, she respects strong Black Men but despises weak ones. I dislike weakness also, so I do not see anything wrong with that.

Anyway, I was once around her during a particular event that we had both attended. I will never forget this day because she had on a really cute dress that made her look even lovelier than she normally looked. Well, on this particular day, she was the most sweetest woman ever! Out of her professional attire, she was simply in her true element, and she looked really beautiful in it. Every time I looked at her, I saw feminine Black beauty and love oozing from her. She could not even control it. Ever since, whenever I see her, even if she is in one hundred percent professional mode, I still think of the person she is in her true element. I never view her as anything other than a loving, good-natured, Beautiful Black Woman. She is a bitch to other people but a goddess to me.

A long time ago, I would have taken one look at all of these Black Women and found myself disinterested in each of them, because I was still a baby in my thinking, so to speak. But, now that I am fully awakened to the innate beauty and loving nature of the Black Woman, my perception of all Black Women, even those who have completely lost the loving part of themselves, is usually favorable. And I oftentimes wish that I could replicate my own perception and place it into the minds of all other Black Men who have dissimilar perceptions but, unfortunately, I cannot. So I just do the best that I can through my actions to inspire Black Men to look beneath Black Women's exteriors and focus on the beauty and loving nature within them. If Black Men start doing this, relationships between Black Men and Black Women will become fruitful.

I was just talking to one of my Black male associates, a really intelligent brother named Terry Perryman, about the loving nature of the Black Woman. I asked him,

"In your opinion, what comes to mind when you think about the loving nature of the Black Woman?" He then seemed to go into a zone during his lengthy response to my question. As he talked about Black Women, his countenance beamed brightly, and his entire demeanor communicated a message that seemed to say, "Man, I *love* me some Black Women! They are the most wonderful beings in all the world!" Some of the most memorable things he said in response to my question, though, were: (1) The Black Woman is the most desired woman in the world; and (2) the Black Woman is the sweetest woman in the world, but she can become the *meanest* woman in the world, if one makes her that way. Allow me to briefly address these responses for one moment, because Terry truly made some important points.

When one truly thinks about it, the Black Woman *is* the most desired woman in the world. Just look at the music industry, for example. Black Women dominate it on many levels. Through their music and style, they are setting new trends that almost all other women want to follow. Women desire the Black Woman's style, elegance, flavor, and grace. And many non-Black men are the same, despite how much they may try to deny it. I was just recently reading a book titled *Bible Legacy of the Black Race* and, in it, the author, a Black Woman by the name of Joyce Andrews, is discussing, among other things, how Black Women of ancient Egypt were glorified by all the world because of their amazing beauty and grace. So this has been going on for millennia. This explains why, during slavery, so many of the slavemasters were so adamant about having sex with Black female slaves. The reason so many of us are not dark-skinned like our African ancestors is that some slavemaster somewhere on a plantation desired a Black

Woman so much that he flat out raped her, unable to control his lust. Usually, he did not even desire his *own* woman that much. I myself have even seen racist Klansmen, and racist descendants of Klansmen, cheat on their wives with the Black Women they desired. I am *still* seeing it today, racist red-necks pursuing the very Black Women they call "niggers" in secret. The point is that the Black Woman is desired on every level imaginable, be it sexual or otherwise. This is not by accident—her desirable qualities are God-given gifts. And these gifts are simply a part of her nature. Therefore, Stupid Black Men need to learn from this and realize that the reason so many people desire or desire to be like Black Women is that the Black Woman is beautiful and loving. It seems as if Black Men are the only ones who cannot see this.

Terry's second point about Black Women being the sweetest women in the world is also true. I look at Beautiful Black Women like Oprah, Michelle Obama, and Maya Angelou and feel nothing but love for them because they exude sweetness. And every Black person I know can point out at least one sweet Black Woman in his or her family. Jamie Foster Brown, the *Sister 2 Sister* publisher I mentioned earlier, falls into this sweet category as well. I dare *all* my readers to flip through one of her magazines in search of a photo that depicts her in a state of non-sweetness. You will not find any, because she is *always* looking and being sweet whenever she is doing whatever it is that she is doing. She is passionate about everything she does and is always spreading love, cheer, and wisdom to others. She exemplifies sweetness, and all Black Women have this same sweetness inside of them. Some Black Women have definitely discovered the sweetness within then, and others who do not exude sweetness just have not discovered it yet. But, still, it lies there at the core of their nature, waiting to be awakened. I understand this, but so many other Black Men in this country do not. And this is why they so often fail in their relationships with

Black Women. Ignorant of the Black Woman's nature, they take Black Women's sweetness for granted. This sometimes angers Black Women so much that they attempt to replace their sweetness with an attitude of nastiness. Thus, the sweetest woman in the world becomes the meanest women in the world. Therefore, it is imperative that Stupid Black Men start acknowledging and appreciating the loving nature of the Beautiful Black Woman. It is time for Stupid Black Men to become "unstupid." Stupid Black Man, "unstupefy" yourself! If you refuse to do so, you will run the risk of losing your Beautiful Black Woman forever, which we will discuss in the following chapter.

Black Men, let me tell you something. Right now, you are not reading the words of a fool. Though I am young, I am wise. But I have not always been this way. At one time, I was *stupid,* with a capital "S." And I am not some random dude who asked a few people a few questions, did a little research, and decided to write a book. I have *dwelled* in stupidity. I have broken a lot of hearts. I have run a lot of Beautiful Black Women away. So I am writing from experience. I was once a player, a pimp, *and* an abuser. I even once despised my own women, but now I love them to death. If *I* can change *my* perception, just imagine what *you* can do. Your Beautiful Black Woman needs you. It is time to man up and handle your business, to take your loving Black Woman into your arms and love her like she needs to be loved. So stop running from her loving nature. *Embrace* it!

Beautiful Black Brothers, have you ever seen a Koala bear, how beautiful and sweet it is, how it always wants to hug on stuff? Well, that is your Beautiful Black Woman, always there yearning to hug you with all of her sweetness. Have you ever seen love bugs during mating season, flying through the air while making love, caught up in the rapture of pure delight? Well, that is your

Beautiful Black Goddess and you flying through life together on the winds of inseparable love! Your woman is a seed, and love is her water. If you pour the contents of your heart onto her, then she will blossom into a beautiful flower that will provide you with happiness for the rest of your days. What kind of man would not want such a flower?

Think about Mother Nature. She is so powerful that man, despite all of his efforts to do so, cannot control Her. No man is strong enough to withstand the force of Her hurricane. No from of technology upon the earth can put an end to Her mighty tornado. And any man foolish enough to doubt Her mighty power does so at his own risk. Now think about Beautiful Black Love. It is so powerful that Black Men, no matter how strong they think they are, eventually bow down to its omnipotence. No Black Man is macho enough to resist it once he encounters it. No other kind of love can even be compared to it. And any Black Man stupid enough to doubt its potency is a fool. Instead of being a fool, why not become a fool in love, which would put an end to such foolishness?

The loving nature of the Black Woman is both seen and unseen, but if you continue blinding yourself with ignorance, my Brother, the seen will become just as unseen as the unseen. Open your eyes and look at your Beautiful Black Woman. I mean, *really look*. Peer into her soul. If her loving nature is visible to you, then become one with that nature. But if it is not visible, then this means that it is your duty as a Black Man to put your hand into the depths of her sweetness and pull it out. If you fail to do so, then you fail both her *and* yourself. So do not fail at Beautiful Black Love—be a winner at it. *Cherish* your woman. The universe is full of great places to take her. Put her first and you become her hero, her savior. Now is the perfect time for her to see what you are made of. Beautiful and loving is the Black Woman's nature!

Chapter Twelve
Ugly Black Hate

In the last chapter, while discussing and elaborating on the loving nature of the Beautiful Black Woman, I mentioned an associate of mine, Terry, who, in his response to a question I posed regarding the Black Woman's nature, said that the Black Woman is the sweetest woman in the world but can become the meanest woman in the world, if one makes her that way. In that chapter, I also stated that, if the Black Man does not become "unstupid" by "unstupefying" himself, then he will run the risk of losing his Beautiful Black Woman forever. Well, in this final chapter, I would like to elaborate on all of this, because Black Men's stupidity is so outrageous nowadays that Black Women are fleeing Black Men in record numbers. So this truly needs to be addressed.

The theme of Beautiful Black Love has been present throughout this entire book. We have gone into detail about BBL, discussed what has to be done in order for us to conserve it, but we have also yet to fully touch on or address BBL's opposite—Ugly Black hate (UBH). Thus, let us do so now.

UBH occurs when Black Men take Beautiful Black Love for granted over an extended period of time, causing Black Women to become so fed up with all of the Black Man's bullshit that she no longer wants anything to do with him. And, in her endeavors to flee the presence of the Black Man, she seeks love elsewhere and sometimes does things that, were she not driven by Ugly

Black Hate, she would not normally do. The decisions she makes, though they may seem to be decisions of deliberate choice, are simply and only the effects of UBH. In fact, because one's decisions dictate one's actions, and one's actions affect one's life, these decisions are thus the *primary* effect of UBH. Here are some of the decisions that are caused by Ugly Black Hate:

- Black Women decide to enter interracial relationships, not to find true love, but rather as payback, to revenge themselves against the Black Men who did not appreciate them.
- Black Women become bitter and choose to make their dissatisfaction with Black Men known by talking badly about them, depicting them negatively.
- As mentioned earlier, Black Women decide to turn to lesbianism in search of the BBL that they were not able to experience with Black Men, because of Black Men's stupidity.
- Black Women make the drastic mistake of choosing to believe that, in no form or fashion, they do not need Black Men.

Of course, these are not the only decisions that Black Women make when they are driven by Ugly Black Hate. However, after studying Black Women and Black relationships for so long, I believe that the above mentioned decisions are the most common. Let us now elaborate on each of them.

Interracial Relationships as Payback

As I have already made clear in Chapter Nine, because love does not come in colors, I absolutely support interracial relationships—if they are entered for the right reasons, with real interest and sincerity. But, when someone who does not have a genuine interest in interracial relationships just enters them for all the wrong reasons, then this is something that I seriously have a problem with, especially when this someone is a woman who enters such relationships as payback. This is just one of the things that happens, however, when stupid men do stupid things to their women.

In the Black world, when a Black Woman goes outside of her race as payback, she knows that this will make a lot of Black Men angry, especially if the man she chooses as her revenge tool is white. She knows that there is still a lot of racial tension in this country between Blacks and their former slavemasters, so she uses this tension to her advantage. And, oftentimes, this devious tactic works. She is pleased whenever she sees Black Men turning their noses up to her in public when they see her on the arm of the white fellow. But this is not fair to *anyone*, including the white guy, whom she has deceived into believing that what they share is true love. He never even suspects that he is being used as a pawn in her wicked revenge plot. Most Black Women who play this nefarious game get addicted to it and go pass the mark they aimed for. Therefore, their little revenge game ends up lasting a lifetime. The Black Man loses her forever.

Negative Depiction of Black Men

One of the worst things a Black Woman can do is put her business out in the street. Why? Because the street is society, society dictates overall public opinion, and public opinion dictates how people treat one another. Black Women who are driven by Ugly Black Hate know that putting negative things out in public about themselves would cause them to be treated negatively by others, which is something that they do not want to experience. To get back at Black men, though, they say all kinds of bad things about them so that they can find pleasure in seeing Black Men squirm when society takes the bait and starts treating Black Men unfairly. And most of the negative things such women say about Black Men in public are outright false. These are oftentimes the kinds of Black Women who go around complaining about Black Men all day, saying things such as, "Black men are no good," "Black men are lazy and don't want to do anything with themselves," and "Black men are dogs who cannot be trusted." Society picks up on these negative depictions and people actually start believing this. And, when the bitter Black Woman sees this, she feels good because this gives her the opportunity to try to show society that she is somehow better than the Black Man. In her attempts to place herself above the Black Man, a wedge is formed between the two of them. She ends up losing herself to her own thirst for revenge, and he ends up womanless.

The Turn to Lesbianism

Because America is a free country and I respect the constitutional rights awarded to all American citizens, I am neither homophobic nor do I look down on others because of their sexual preferences. However, I do believe that it is wrong for one to change his or her sexual preference simply because he or she failed at love with people of the opposite sex, especially when such a person gravitates toward the same sex *only* in search of the Beautiful Black Love that was never experienced with the partner of the opposite sex. The reason I believe this is wrong is that the BBL that I speak of is reserved for woman and man. This is not to say that woman and woman or man and man cannot experience real love, because same-sex couples find love all the time. But the love shared between a woman and a man is a more intense kind of love.

Anyway, when Black Women enter lesbianism in search of a kind of love that only a man can give them, though they may indeed find a kind of love that another woman can give them, the possibility of BBL shared between her and man no longer exists. She therefore goes about her life either in pursuit of or experiencing an entirely different kind of love. As she gets lost in her new pursuit, the Black Man becomes lost without her.

The Black Man as not Needed

The reason that Black Women's belief that they do not need Black Men is a drastic mistake is that it encourages them to perpetuate an "independent woman" attitude that distances them from their Black Men. There is nothing wrong with being independent and doing things for oneself, but when a woman begins believing that a Black Man cannot do *anything* for her, she is sadly mistaken. Nothing that is not a man can replace a man. If the Creator were to kill off men and populate the earth with only females, the earth's population would die off because, without men, there would be no procreation. But Ugly Black Hate is so powerful that it blinds Black Women, and they become convinced that Black Men serve no real purpose.

Another kind of Black Woman who is driven by UBH is one who believes that the Black Man, rather than serving *no* purpose, serves a *limited* purpose in the independent Black Woman's world. Therefore, this kind of woman may date Black Men, but her association with these men usually goes no further than sex. And she only deals with Black Men because she believes that, though there are definitely some hot non-Black men out there in the world, only a Brother can put it down right in the bedroom. A vibrator does not suffice. This kind of woman usually likes to pay for the meals on dates and cover all significant date-related expenses because she does not want the Black Man she is dating to do anything for her outside of the bedroom. This is just another way of telling him that she can do without him. In her mind, she is saying, "I got this!" This may seem cool to her, but all this does is pushes her farther away from the Black Man emotionally. Eventually, she becomes lost, both to herself and to the Black Man. But this is not her fault—it is his, because his stupidity drove her to this point.

All of these things discussed above are the primary things that Black Women do when they, after becoming completely fed up with Black Men's stupidity, become driven by Ugly Black Hate. And, if Stupid Black Men remain stupid, then there will be a serious increase in UBH-related behavior. Black Women all over this country will begin entering interracial relationships as payback, depicting Black Men negatively, turning to lesbianism, and believing that Black Men serve no real purpose in their world. Consequently, Beautiful Black Love will become an endangered feeling and experience on the verge of extinction, and all of the problems that Black people already have in this country will get worse. All of this and more will happen because of the absence of BBL and the prevalence of UBH. This is why it is extremely important for Stupid Black Men to wake the hell up. If they do not, then we as a people are doomed.

I would like to close this chapter by revealing to you, my beloved readers, in full, one conversation I had with a Beautiful Black Woman about a month ago regarding the subject of Ugly Black Hate. This woman, who we will call Trisha, is currently single and transitioning into a state of UBH because she is fed up with all of the stupidity she has had to endure in her dealings with Stupid Black Men. I chose this particular woman because her story reflects all of the things I have just mentioned in this chapter about the four primary decisions that Black Women make when they become driven by Ugly Black Hate. I was unable to have this conversation recorded, but I am an extensive note taker, so I have all of the information I need to reconstruct this conversation to the best of my ability. Black Men, pay attention, because this is what happens when we allow our stupidity to push our Beautiful Black Women away.

Trisha

Me: "Hi, Trish! It's been a while since I've seen or talked to you. Did you get the questionnaire I had sent to you by mail regarding the Ugly Black Hate subject that I'll be addressing in my new book I told you about?"

Trisha: "Yes, hon, I got it. I've just been so busy out here trying to stay independent and take care of *me*, you know. So I haven't had time to sit down and respond to all of your questions. But I *do* appreciate you considering me for possible publication in your book. Boy, you are going to make some Black Woman out here very happy someday after you get out! You still single?"

Me: "I see you still call everybody 'hon.' Anyway, don't worry about filling out the questionnaire, because we can discuss all of that now if you like. And, as for me considering you, girl, you know I love my Black Sisters! Plus, I feel like your story should be told in your *own* words. So you know I had to keep you in mind. We don't talk often, but you're still my girl. Oh, and yes, I'm still single—technically. But there is a particular someone in my life and it's getting kind of serious between us. I think she may just be the one. But, anyway, what about you—you still single, too?"

Trisha: "You know me, always going through some bullshit with these stupid ass men out here. So I'm still single. But after we talked the last time—how long ago was that? About a year?"

Me: "About a year and a half."

Trisha: "Oh, well, anyway, after we talked the last time, I met a really nice guy who turned out to be an idiot like my ex before him, and my ex before him, and my ex before that. We did our thing for almost a whole year, and then things just got crazy. One of his old loves popped up, and he started acting all funny and suspicious. I got jealous because I had fallen in love with him by this time, and I told him about it, to reassure me that we're still good and I had nothing to worry about. He said everything was all good and, like a fool, I believed him. But she had a hold on him. So one day I followed him on his day off, and I caught her and him together going into a hotel. I didn't have no beef with her, so I got out my car and confronted just him in front of her in the hotel. That's when he told me it was over between us. Just like that, it was over. I left, then came back to pay one of the housekeeper chics to keep an eye out and call me if they had sex. I left again but came back when she called me. Then I got her to open the door to their room, and I burst in on them having sex. We got into a big fight. It was crazy."

Me: "Damn. He was stupid. I'm sorry you had to go through that. What did you do next?"

Trisha: "Well, that was the end of us. But I was so mad, not just at him but *all* Black Men, that I did some crazy stuff just to make him mad."

Me: "What kind of crazy stuff?"

Trisha: "You won't believe me if I tell you."

Me: "Yes, I will. And you know I won't ever judge you, especially if it's something slutty, because you know I used to be a *dirty* male slut back in my day!"

Trisha: (Laughs) "I fucked his friends—all of them. The Black ones, the white one, even his lesbian homegirl. That was my first time ever being with a white dude and another woman, but I had to get him back. And, I must admit, it actually felt *good*. He was, like, 'Whatever,' when he found out about me and his black friend, the dude. But when he found out about me and the white guy, he went *berserk*! And he just went stone crazy when he found out what happened between me and his homegirl. I recorded it on camera and mailed it to his sister's house, and she showed it to him. Now I have his attention. I went around his neighborhood telling everybody what I did, and now he can't even go anywhere without people looking at him funny, knowing how I played him. And I don't feel bad about it either. *He* played *me*, and I played *him*. He got what he deserved. I even told everybody about his little erectile dysfunction problems. But it feels good to be single again, because I don't have time to keep playing games with these men, giving my heart away, only to have it broken in return. I'm so tired of their games. I'm seriously considering the whole woman on woman thing because, with women, at least I won't have to go through all the bullshit I have to go through with men. That's how I'm feeling right now, Cornell. Seriously."

Me: "I know that you're hurt and you're venting right now, but don't let all that stupidity make you give up on Beautiful Black Love. All the things that you have gone through with Stupid Black Men are only preparing you for the true love you'll experience someday. When you find that love, you won't want to lose it, because you won't want to run the risk of ending up with another Stupid Black Man. I know it's hard, love, but be patient. Let your desire for love guide you. If you do that, you're going to be okay."

Trisha: "I hope you're right."

Me: "I am. But, anyway, I have to go. I wish I could stay and talk to you, but you know how things are with my schedule and all of that. But it was nice talking to you. As soon as my book gets published, I'll have a free copy mailed to you—if I can track you down! Until then, keep your head up, and *never* stop believing in love. And always remember that, in the world of relationships, there is no greater love than the love shared between the Black Man and the Black Woman. Oh, and take care of yourself!"

Love Letter to the Beautiful Black Woman— A Lyric Poem

Dear Beautiful Black Woman,

As I sit here pondering you, pondering love, I am reminded of our first encounter. You have been superior to me from the beginning! When I was simply nonexistent nothingness, you were a beautiful entity of existent somethingness. It seemed like magic, the way we met. There you were, lying there, your valley wide open. I had been fighting against the current of your stream for nine months in that valley! You used the powerful force of your inner wind to push me out of your valley and onto dry land, and we fell in love as soon as we lay our eyes on each other. Since that time, I have gotten to know you on *all kinds* of levels. You have acted as my nurturer, my guardian, and my teacher. At times, I could not comprehend your nurturing, guidance, and instruction, so I rebelled against that which I did not understand. But you were patient with me and welcomed me with open arms when I finally began to "get" you and came running into your embrace. Look at us now, our souls entwined in passion. I now know you on another level that consists of many other levels.

I know you spiritually because we are both animated by the same force that animates all living beings in the universe. We have both sat at the right hand of God. I am God's son, and you are God's daughter, yet you are both God's goddess *and* mine. You have ascended into Heaven, and I have descended into hell in order to likewise ascend into the heavens. We are different but one and the same in Spirit. We swap words that are in accordance with the Scriptures. I am you. You are me. Flesh, we are One underneath!

I know you mentally because our thoughts are connected by hemispheres. I am predominately one hemisphere, and you are the same. But we exist inside of each other on both the left and right sides of the brain. You inherited your mind directly from the Creator, even though I lied and said that you inherited it from me through one of my ribs by way of the Creator. And I inherited my mind from you by way of the Creator, even though I lied and told myself that I inherited it directly from Him, like you. Our personalities lie together in the bed of thought. Therefore, we blanket each other with the notion of each other!

I know you emotionally because we are both pieces of consciousness that involve feeling. We are both raindrops of sensibility that storm down on each other in ways that feel both good and bad. I am sometimes an earthquake that causes an ocean to flow down your face. And you are sometimes a tremor that causes a river to flow down from mine. Other times we bless each other with rainbows during the downpour of our rain. I feel you like you feel me. We are both zooming up and down, round and round, zigzagging on this rollercoaster called emotion. And we are holding each other tight!

I know you physically because I dwelled inside of you, and dove *out* of you, during the infantile stage of my physical existence. I have slept atop of your stomach, drunken nectar from your breasts, been hugged by your arms, and lovingly caressed by your hands. I can distinguish you easily because you have a body like no other. I know the beauty of your lips, the magnificence of your nose. Girl, I can spot your booty from a mile away!

I know you sexually because you are my deep sea, and I am your black stallion, your steed. I dive into you and swim to the very depths of your waters. I seek to *drown* inside of you. You climb on top of me and ride me like a cowgirl. I buck and you fall off then get back on, loving the way I leap with arched back and land with head low and forelegs stiff. We do more than take each other to ecstasy without taking Ecstasy. We bring each other to climax in a climatic frenzy that only begins at the ending of round one's culmination. We are the poster children of procreation. I run my tongue across the length and width of your body as if it is measuring tape, as I wonder how much pleasure you can take. I run my palms across your thighs. I am considered a poem in your eyes. You decipher me in the nude, love. I am, like, "Oooh, this is *true* love!"

I know I have not always been the man that I am supposed to be. I know I have made *tons* of mistakes. I have been stupid. But do not think for a moment that I do not love you, because you are the *only* woman on earth I truly desire, more than the dolphins in the sea desire water, more than the birds in the air desire the wind! I knew not what I did when I did what I did but said that I did not do. And I mean what I say when I say what I say about me loving you, because I do! You gave birth to humanity when we sat on that throne. My *love* impregnated you, not my seed. We played in that garden, no loincloth, no leaves. Our love existed *way* before Adam and Eve!

I hate to see you crying, baby. I am so sorry for causing those tears. I was so caught up in my own ignorance, a spider stuck in my own web, that I did not consider your feelings. Please, please, forgive me! My Nubian Goddess, my Kemetian Queen, let us get back to fulfilling our dreams! Let us go back to the days of tranquility. Let us go back to nights of no pain. Let us continue to feel what it is like to be free from the knife of heartbreak and mind games. Tell me you love me, that you still need me. Slap away my stupidity and then kiss my face! I put no one above you.

I want you. Believe me! That is the way it is with me. I love how you *taste*!

Ooooh, Beautiful Black Woman, I love you so much! I love the way your hair rolls up in kinky curls, the way you walk with that sway in your hips. I love your intense passion and emotion. Shit, I love EVERYTHING about you! Close your eyes and imagine us walking together, hand in hand, atop the clouds. I kiss you, pick you up, and then we fall down on all of that softness. Imagine us being able to breathe beneath water without drowning, the two of us walking along the ocean floor, just marveling at all of the beautiful marine creatures as they swim by. That is *peace*. Now open your eyes. I love you so much now that I feel peaceful like that when I think of you in all of your splendor. You make me happy. You are the definition of felicity. You run through my mind and jump rope with my soul. I cannot get enough of you. You are my everything!

I am willing to do whatever is necessary to have you back in my life. Do I have to walk through fire? Do I have to jump from a plane with no parachute? Do I have to bungee jump without a bungee cord? Just say the word, and it is done! I would squeeze into the head of a needle for you. I would wrestle with a lion to earn your forgiveness. I *got* it now: I cannot hurt you without hurting myself. I swear, I will not mess up again. *Hell* with infidelity! *Hell* with domestic violence! I do not want to be stupid anymore. All I want to do is love you . . . love you . . . love you. So, can we please get back to love . . . love . . . love?

As I sit here writing this, I have chills running up and down my spine, because I am speaking from the soul. Though you and I are miles away from each other, separated by distance, we are closer than ever because, in my mind, you are right here beside me. I am looking at you looking back at me. As I write with my right hand, you are holding my left. And you are more beautiful than ever! I want to kiss you so badly! Taste my tongue!

I am talking to every Beautiful Black Woman out there. The one with the broken heart, whose man is cheating on her. The one whose spirit feels broken because her man is beating her. The one who trusted a man who infected her with HIV or AIDS. The one who is in a messed up relationship that seems unfixable. I am talking to you! The one with the dark skin who Stupid Black Men look down upon and say is ugly. The one with the child or children that the father(s) want nothing to do with. The one who is recently divorced after a troubled marriage. The one who is just fed up with the Black Man's crap. I am talking to you! I *love* you! Forgive him! Forgive *me*! Just let Beautiful Black Love rule. If you truly want it, you will find it. All you have to do is believe.

I can sit here all day begging you to forgive me, your Beautiful Black Man, but, if you do not have forgiveness in your heart, all of my words will simply fall on deaf ears. Do not be bitter towards me because of my stupidity. Give me another chance to prove to you that our hearts are destined to move throughout time and space, like whole galaxies do. Let our little heart galaxies travel in unison. Open your heart to me once again. Let us throw stones of renewed kinship at your seemingly impenetrable wall of defense mechanisms until it collapses. Let me un-break your heart and un-cry your tears! I promise that I will never hurt you again. Baby, I promise!

I do not know what else I can say to convince you to take me, your Black Man, back and give Beautiful Black Love another chance, so I will close this letter with the following words: Sometimes it is not the fire that burns but rather the fearful perceptions of the once burned that ignites the creation of burning sensation. If I am an extinguished fire and neither of us are flammable, why fear combustion when I am something you can handle? Let love guide you and you will figure it out! I love you!

Sincerely,
Cornell

About the Author

Cornell Martin, in addition to being a writer, is a trilingual interpreter/translator who spends much of his time breaking communication barriers among the Deaf, hard of hearing, Hispanic, and English-speaking communities. He also holds an Associate degree in General Studies with a concentration in General Business, and is a staff writer/photographer for the *Chainlink Chronicle,* a prison-based publication. Some of his articles have appeared on the front page of the *Daily News,* a local Louisiana newspaper, and featured in the nation of Islam's true to life newspaper *The Final Call.* He has also appeared on television in a news special conducted by well-known WDSU news reporter Rosa Flores. When not writing or interpreting, he can usually be found tutoring Deaf students.

Cornell spends most of his free time reading nonfiction books, exercising, writing screenplays and songs, and kicking it with family and friends. A native of New Orleans' Treme neighborhood, the hub of Black Culture in the Big Easy, he loves discussing the greatness of unparalleled Black world history. But, when it comes to what he loves most, God and the Beautiful Black Woman are at the very top of his list. Cornell also loves to hear from his readers, so anyone who is interested in contacting him should feel free to do so. At the time of publication, the author is currently incarcerated and awaiting his imminent release. His contact information is listed on the Contact the Author page.

Also, in his books, the author loves to write about subjects that most other authors never seem to write about. Therefore, if you are passionate about a subject that you cannot find a book about, or if you are passionate about a subject that you *can* find a book about but the book is not in-depth, then feel free to contact the author and tell him about it. Who knows—his next book may be written about this subject and, if you are interested, you could even become a co-author on this potential project.

Contact the Author

Anyone who is interested in contacting the author can do so in two ways: by mail and email. He prefers snail mail, because letters are more personal. However, whichever option you choose is okay, and your mail will get to him either way.

By Mail

If you intend to use the mailing option, write to the following address:

Cornell Martin #461133
Rayburn Correctional Center
27268 Highway 21N
Angie, LA 70426

By Email

If you intend to use the email option, you will have to do the following:
1. Log on to www.jpay.com
2. Set up an email account (instructions on how to do so are found on the JPay website, and the author's name, prison number, and prison name and location is, for the most part, all you really need to know to set up your JPay email account).

Despite how hectic his schedule is, the author wants you to know that he is *never* too busy for his readers. So, if you decide to write to him, as long as you have a positive attitude, he *will* try his best to write you back. And he also promises that he will try his best to respond to your mail in a timely manner.

The author, Cornell Martin, kissing his beautiful big sister, Shandreka, during a very special visit. Nothing can describe the love that he has for her, but this kiss is just one of the many ways that he shows his love! The beautiful little brown girl you see is his niece, Daneisha. He loves her just as much as well!

REAL

LOVE

NEVER

DIES!

Cornell and his close friend, Christopher Pelican, on College Graduation Day, January 2012. This accomplishment is just one of many ways that these men are proving that rehabilitation is real! The sky is the limit!

REAL

FRIENDSHIP

NEVER

FADES!

BEAUTIFUL

BLACK

WOMAN,

I LOVE YOU!!!

I LOVE YOU!!!

STUPID

BLACK

MAN,

WAKE UP!

WAKE UP!